Approaching Interdisciplinarity: Archaeology, History and the Study of Early Medieval Britain, c.400-1100

Edited by

Zoë L. Devlin
Caroline N. J. Holas-Clark

BAR British Series 486
2009

Published in 2016 by
BAR Publishing, Oxford

BAR British Series 486

Approaching Interdisciplinarity: Archaeology, History and the Study of Early Medieval Britain, c.400-1100

© The editors and contributors severally and the Publisher 2009

The authors' moral rights under the 1988 UK Copyright,
Designs and Patents Act are hereby expressly asserted.

All rights reserved. No part of this work may be copied, reproduced, stored,
sold, distributed, scanned, saved in any form of digital format or transmitted
in any form digitally, without the written permission of the Publisher.

ISBN 9781407304410 paperback
ISBN 9781407321493 e-format
DOI https://doi.org/10.30861/9781407304410
A catalogue record for this book is available from the British Library

BAR Publishing is the trading name of British Archaeological Reports (Oxford) Ltd.
British Archaeological Reports was first incorporated in 1974 to publish the BAR
Series, International and British. In 1992 Hadrian Books Ltd became part of the BAR
group. This volume was originally published by Archaeopress in conjunction with
British Archaeological Reports (Oxford) Ltd / Hadrian Books Ltd, the Series
principal publisher, in 2009. This present volume is published by BAR Publishing,
2016.

BAR

PUBLISHING

BAR titles are available from:

BAR Publishing
122 Banbury Rd, Oxford, OX2 7BP, UK
EMAIL info@barpublishing.com
PHONE +44 (0)1865 310431
FAX +44 (0)1865 316916
www.barpublishing.com

Contents

Julian D. Richards
Preface   1

Alex Woolf
A dialogue of the deaf and the dumb: archaeology, history and philology   3

Morn Capper
The practical implications of interdisciplinary approaches: research in
Anglo-Saxon East Anglia   10

Caroline Holas-Clark
Archaeology, history and economics: exploring everyday life in Anglian Deira   24

Zoë L. Devlin
The end of Anglo-Saxon furnished burial: an interdisciplinary perspective   28

Mike F. Reed
Sculpture and lordship in Late Saxon Suffolk: the evidence of Ixworth   38

Sharon A. Greene
Reassessing remoteness: Ireland's western off-shore islands in the early medieval period   47

Michael Garcia
Romans go home? An archaeological and historical exploration of the cult of saints in
late antique Britain   55

Sarah Boss
Alcuin of York on wisdom and Mary: texts and buildings   62

Zoë L. Devlin
Approaching interdisciplinarity   72

Preface

In November 2006 a conference was held at the Centre for Medieval Studies in the University of York on interdisciplinary studies in the early medieval period, covering the period *c*. AD 400-1100. The Centre for Medieval Studies at York is a well-established centre for interdisciplinary postgraduate teaching and research, drawing upon scholars in the Departments of Archaeology, English and Related Literature, History and History of Art. It prides itself upon its interdisciplinary team teaching and all its research students are co-supervised by academics from at least two of the parent departments. However, staff are frequently challenged to define what true interdisciplinarity is. This is a particular problem for the Early Middle Ages when any sources are scarce and rarely relate to the same issues or themes. Indeed, archaeologists are often chastised for trying to relate the chance survivals of material evidence to the chance events recorded in documentary sources in a period when both are scarce. Whilst later medievalists may even have the luxury of tax returns or rolls which relate to excavated buildings, the early medievalist is forced to undertake interdisciplinary research at a more abstract level. The greatest challenge is often to pose the right question, so that different categories of evidence can each be brought to bear on the same problem.

In an attempt to address some of the issues faced by interdisciplinary studies in the Early Middle Ages, Zoë Devlin and Caroline Holas-Clark, then both undertaking doctoral research involving both archaeological and historical sources, organised a day conference at the King's Manor in York. With the exception of the keynote address by Alex Woolf they deliberately invited new researchers within interdisciplinary studies who were each grappling with case studies of their own. The collection of papers they have gathered here reflects some of the excitement of the meeting and the enthusiasm of a new generation of medievalists to tackle these issues.

The papers are grouped into two sections. The contributions by Alex Woolf, Morn Capper and Caroline Holas-Clark all focus on the practical issues surrounding interdisciplinary research. Woolf opens the volume by examining the history of interdisciplinary studies on the early medieval period and comments on how developments in theory, the legacy of nineteenth century scholarship and the administrative structures of universities have inadvertently undermined the relationship between history and archaeology. Woolf argues that we should stop dividing ourselves into archaeologists and historians and instead look upon ourselves as a wide range of specialists in studying the past. Only by drawing upon the expertise from all relevant fields, including philology, can we hope to gain a fully rounded understanding of the past.

For Woolf, acknowledging and drawing upon the range of specialist skills available within history and archaeology is key to improving communication and enhancing understanding between the two disciplines. Skills are also an area of concern for both Capper and Holas-Clark, who discuss the impact that the need to gain new skills has on the scope and timescale of an interdisciplinary research project. Capper, whose research project focused on the identities of the midland kingdoms in the period *c*.700-*c*.900, argues that an interdisciplinary approach must be justified, not least because the time spent gaining the skills necessary to do justice to the available evidence means that the time spent working on the project itself is necessarily shortened. For Holas-Clark, who reflects on her interdisciplinary study of the economy of Deira, 700-867, a 'truly interdisciplinary approach is a gamble', involving the investment of a considerable amount of time in acquiring the skills necessary to evaluate specialist reports, time that might otherwise be spent examining primary sources. Capper and Holas-Clark also discuss how the use of more than one type of evidence and methodology can lead to compromise in other areas, such as the geographical or temporal scope of the project. Capper also considers the question of whether an interdisciplinary approach should incorporate a distinct interdisciplinary methodology and concludes that research questions can only be formulated and answered within the confines of a single discipline. An interdisciplinary approach therefore lies in combining the results of disciplinary analysis, based on complementary research questions.

Despite the issues raised by interdisciplinary research, Woolf, Capper and Holas-Clark are convinced of its huge potential and the remainder of the papers aim to provide examples of successful interdisciplinary research. Zoë L. Devlin considers whether documentary material in the form of late Anglo-Saxon wills can be used to provide contextual evidence for the end of furnished burial. She argues that the wills reveal both continuities and changes in people's perceptions of personal belongings in the context of death during this period and concludes that the long-term process of Christianisation led to the deceased's possessions being retained by those with a duty to pray for them rather than being interred in the grave. Here, the archaeological and documentary evidence are examined for what they each reveal about attitudes to objects and the results lead to an alternative perspective on changes in the archaeological record.

Michael F. Reed examines the nature of late Anglo-Saxon lordship in Suffolk, combining iconographic, archaeological and textual approaches to create an integrated social history. By considering the evidence gained from sculpture and archaeological finds at the local level against the background provided by contemporary documentary sources, he is able to argue that the assertion of lordly status and social identity is influenced by both context and medium in which it is expressed. While sculptural motifs are conservative, lack

Scandinavian elements, and are intended to proclaim the patron's lordly status within an ecclesiastical context, bridle fittings and stirrup mounts indicate the assertion of a Danish identity in secular contexts. The evidence from surviving texts on the ecclesiastical reforms of the period and the strong Danish culture at Cnut's court indicate reasons for these different expressions of identity at different times.

Sharon A. Greene's paper reassesses our perception of Ireland's western off-shore islands in the early medieval period by questioning the idea that islands were necessarily considered remote or separate by people living on them at the time. She considers the idea of 'separateness' from the mainland in terms of geology, environment and culture and uses the textual evidence to question archaeologists' assumptions about remoteness. While there is a tendency to consider these islands as remote and empty places, both the palaeoenvironmental evidence and the documentary sources suggest that this was not the case. Rather there was a good deal of travel between the islands and the mainland and the sea was an aid to communication rather than a barrier. Greene concludes that terms like 'remote' should be applied more sparingly with an understanding of perceptions drawn from contemporary textual sources rather than being based on modern assumptions.

Michael Garcia discusses saints' cults in Britain *c.*300-700 AD, exploring the evidence for cults other than St Alban's via several approaches: historical, archaeological and interdisciplinary. He presents the evidence offered by textual sources, as well as the archaeological evidence which might corroborate these sources. He discusses what an archaeologically determined approach might look like, but also shows how an interdisciplinary approach might reconcile these methods. The implication is that we must use archaeological evidence too to look at saints' cults because there is such a paucity of documentary evidence. Garcia concludes that an interdisciplinary approach enables us to ask questions that we can't ask of each type of source on its own and that the evidence of one enables us to critique the interpretations we get from the other.

Finally, Sarah Boss uses both archaeological and textual evidence to examine Christopher Norton's suggestion that Alcuin's church dedicated to Holy Wisdom was located where the present York Minster Chapter House stands. She relates the hypothetical building to the surrounding area and considers how it would have fit in to the early medieval landscape. Boss also considers the possible influence of centrally planned buildings on the continent in its construction as well as the importance of number and shape for the architecture of sacred buildings. Altogether, an interdisciplinary approach gives a fuller understanding of the context for the building of Alcuin's church along with a better understanding of the early medieval sense of place and of the relationship between architecture and religious texts.

Overall, each of these chapters contributes to interdisciplinary scholarship but they also illustrate some of the difficulties and frustrations, particularly in the study of the Early Middle Ages. Nonetheless interdisciplinary research is now much more in favour with research funders and universities are becoming more creative about finding ways to break down barriers put up by departmental divisions. There is still a long way to go but hopefully this volume will provide a basis for further discussion.

Professor Julian D Richards, York Jan 2009
Co-Director, Centre for Medieval Studies, University of York, 2003-06.

A dialogue of the deaf and the dumb: archaeology, history and philology

Alex Woolf

Part I

My Name is Alex Woolf. I am an archaeologist. The good news is that I am in recovery. I have not picked up a trowel for nearly ten years.

My original plan, as a student, was to become an Anglo-Saxonist. Although my degree, at the University of Sheffield (graduated 1989), was in Medieval History and Medieval English I was also able to take Archaeology as an outside subject in my first year and the early medieval modules within the Archaeology degree were available to History students. I also took part in excavations during all the vacations and attended research seminars in the Archaeology Department. I hung about there so much that many of the staff assumed I was an archaeology student who just didn't happen to be taking their modules.

It had seemed to me that this approach would allow me to develop a range of skills and a knowledge base that would equip me to deal with the Anglo-Saxon past in the best possible fashion. Unfortunately I learned fairly rapidly that this was not to be the case. Even as an undergraduate I found that almost identical essay questions had to be answered differently for a tutor in Archaeology than for a tutor in History. The 'Anglo-Saxon Invasions' were a case in point. Richard Hodges, my Archaeology tutor, has actually gone into print, in *The Anglo-Saxon Achievement*, saying that there need have been no Anglo-Saxon immigrants to account for the transformation of Late Antique Britain (1989, 190). This was the late 1980s when the 'immobilist' or 'anti-Invasion' ideology was in its first flush of youth with Southampton graduates, ultimately the students of Colin Renfrew, such as Hodges and Chris Arnold (1984) dominating the more exciting end of Anglo-Saxon archaeology.

These 'immobilists' had misunderstood the warning salvo fired by Graham Clark's seminal *Antiquity* paper of 1966, 'The Invasion Hypothesis in British Archaeology', and the ripples spreading from the translation of linear B (which is why Renfrew's role is so significant). Clark began his article by stating unequivocally that he believed that '[e]ven the last 2,000 years have witnessed three major phases of invasion and numerous small infiltrations and there is every reason to think that prehistoric Britain must also have experienced incursions of a kind' (1966, 173). At the heart of Clark's critique of the invasion hypothesis was *not* scepticism about the facts of invasion, conquest and the displacement of populations (no European who had lived through the first half of the twentieth century could have had doubts about the reality of such phenomena), but an anxiety about what he called the 'invasion neurosis' which sought to explain all cultural innovation as the result of invasion. This 'neurosis' had led his predecessors to build up a succession of invasions of Britain, going far back into prehistory, simply to explain the appearance of new forms of material expression. Sometimes such forms could be seen to be so close to Continental models as to warrant the suggestion that they might represent the 'extension of the influence' of a pre-existing culture group, but at other times, as with Peterborough Ware (ibid., 173-6), there were no clear precursors anywhere. Clark wondered whether British prehistorians 'went out of their way to ascribe every good thing about their early past to foreign influences, if not indeed to foreign conquerors', as part of an attempt to legitimise British invasion and domination of less complex polities in the nineteenth and twentieth centuries (ibid., 172).

Clark was also critical of Christopher Hawkes' 'ABC of the British Iron Age' (1959), which had attempted to equate the last major phase of cultural transformation in pre-Roman Britain with the invasions by portions of the Belgae. Caesar had indeed mentioned Belgic invasions in the not too distant past in his account of his own attempts to conquer the island (*DBG* V.), but subsequent refining of the chronology of the archaeological phenomena indicated, however, that Hawkes' 'Belgic' Iron Age C material post-dated Caesar's own time and thus could not be related to the invasions that he had mentioned, or indeed to subsequent invasions which would surely have been noted by Classical observers now that the Romans controlled Gaul. One can further strengthen Clark's case here by adding that the three Late Pre-Roman Iron Age tribes in Britain which bore identical names to peoples in or near the Belgic part of Gaul – the Parisii, the Atrebates and the Belgae – did not occupy territories that have produced significant quantities of 'Iron Age C' material. It is thus likely that while Belgic invasions did happen they left no recognisable archaeological record, and that, subsequently, a period of significant Continental influence on some native British tribes occurred without any large-scale movement of people (Cunliffe 1995, 63-4).

Clark's message then was not that invasions did not happen, though this view is often attributed to him, but that Archaeology, as a discipline, was not best suited to identifying invasions. And so, as so often happens, his academic grandchildren Hodges, Arnold *et al.*, misconstrued his message. Hodges even felt able to state that 'prehistorians have now dismissed the notion of invasions in the Neolithic, Bronze and Iron Ages' (1989, 190), in order to legitimise his own views on the early Anglo-Saxon period. Of course this was not true then, though it seems to some extent to be true now. What

Clark and his colleagues had argued was not that there had been no invasions in the Neolithic, Bronze and Iron Ages, but rather that it was unlikely that Neolithic, Bronze and Iron technology had been brought to these islands by invaders as discrete cultural packages: an entirely different proposition.

As Tim Champion (1990, 215) has pointed out, '[a]ll *prehistoric* migrations .... are .... entirely hypothetical', and within the constraints of the New Archaeology which proclaimed 'the invalidity of the hypothesis which cannot be tested' (*loc. cit.*), the value of the migration as an explanation of culture change collapsed. This is, however, merely an admission of a blind spot in the perspective on the past available to archaeologists and not a demonstration of the non-existence of invasions or even, in some cases, their potential for explaining material culture change. Working in the early historical period, however, *we* are not constrained by the limitations placed on material culture study alone and if other disciplines, historical or philological, can allow us to look into archaeology's blind spots then look into them we must.

Interestingly both Arnold and Hodges (and Higham (1992) seems to have taken his lead from them) trained at the University of Southampton at the time when the Chair of Archaeology at that university was held by Colin (now Lord) Renfrew. Renfrew was himself, during this period, something of a specialist on 'Dark Ages'. At about the time Arnold and Hodges were completing their doctoral research, he was attempting to produce a processualist model to explain the phenomenon (Renfrew 1979 and 1982).

Although, in these early days of the New Archaeology, Renfrew was attempting to produce generally applicable rules governing the collapse of complex societies, he had approached 'Dark Age Studies' via his interest in the development of the Hellenic world. The Greek Dark Ages followed the collapse of the Mycenaean civilisation of the Middle Bronze Age and comprised the Late Bronze Age and Early Iron Age in the Aegean region. In this field of study the period of Renfrew's own days as a student had seen the collapse of a paradigm. The traditional view, constructed from a Culture Historical rationalisation of Classical Greek myths, was that the collapse of the complex literate societies of the Middle Bronze Age which had produced the palaces at sites such as Mycenae, Tiryns and Pylos (as well as on the ruins of earlier Minoan palaces at Knossos and other sites in Crete), had been brought about by barbarian invaders from the North.

Because the destruction of the Bronze Age civilisation seemed so complete it was assumed that these northern barbarians must have effected complete ethnic replacement, and therefore that they must have been responsible for introducing the language that was to become Greek into the region (Renfrew 1987, 57-63). The revelation by Michael Ventris that the Linear B script used on the Mycenaean sites had been used to record a language clearly ancestral to Classical Greek (Chadwick and Ventris 1956) completely destroyed this model. It was left to the post-Ventris generation, including the young Colin Renfrew, to devise a new series of historical models that would explain the collapse of the complex Mycenaean culture, and its replacement with a myriad of barbaric tribal groups, without recourse to large-scale invasions. Renfrew's attempts to transform his preferred explanation of culture change in the Greek Dark Age (e.g. 1969) into a generally applicable rule for Dark Ages *per se* (that is to say, for the collapse of complex societies), seems to have been a defining influence on Arnold and Hodges. Paradoxically, however, the key to this re-analysis of the Greek Dark Age was the recognition of linguistic continuity across it – a feature conspicuous by its absence from the British Dark Age.

The Renfrew school's modelling of Dark Age systems collapse was able, by appropriation of some of the rhetoric of Clark's thesis and by recourse to the avowedly anti-historical politics of the New Archaeology, to win widespread acceptance among prehistorians, while at the same time closing the door on any meaningful dialogue with historians (Arnold 1984, 6-20), who have generally found the documentary evidence for large-scale invasion unassailable. Until recently there had been little attempt to confront this anti-invasionist paradigm head on, partly because the demonstration of the fact of invasions requires, as we have seen, recourse to non-archaeological data, a course of action which leaves its practitioners open to the charge of treating Archaeology as the hand-maid of history and showing themselves to be disloyal to the discipline. More recently Renfrew himself (1987, 5) has sought to distance himself from the more extreme approach claiming '[n]o one is asserting that migrations do not or have not occurred', but as John Hines (1998, 159) has demonstrated it is precisely 'enthusiastic protagonists of this 'New' archaeological approach', Renfrew's following, who have been promoting this position, as the citation from Hodges, made earlier, demonstrates.

Among prehistorians a few cautionary notes have been sounded by serious scholars who should be heeded (e.g. Anthony 1990; Champion 1990 and Kristiansen 1991), but most Anglo-Saxonists have kept their heads below the parapet. Welch, in his English Heritage volume, confined himself to brief comments (1992, 11-12, though see Welch 1985 for a fuller exposition of his views) but it was clear that he recognised that the language question was an insuperable problem for the elite emulation model, which argued that a tiny number of politically significant Germans were responsible for the transformation of Britain into England. As he points out, the elite emulation model looks very like the situation which prevailed in England in the two or three centuries following the Norman conquest of 1066 which did not lead to the adoption of the language of the invaders by the masses. While such a model may be fine for explaining the diffusion of material culture, about which archaeologists are the recognised experts, it should be noted that in most historically attested examples of conquering, minority, elites, such as the Normans in

England or the Langobards in Italy, it was the 'elites' who eventually adopted the language of the masses, albeit somewhat modified. Indeed it is hard to think of a single case in which it can be demonstrated, unequivocally, that the reverse occurred.

Helena Hamerow (1994), in a more significant discussion of the migration issue, confined herself to an indication of the methodological and empirical flaws in the arguments of the anti-invasionists, apparently reserving judgement on the question of whether their inability to marshal the evidence to support their case means that they are fundamentally wrong about the past or simply poor practitioners of their art. One comes away from her article, however, feeling that her sympathies are definitely with the mass-migration lobby. John Hines, whose work has focused on migration, has largely avoided the issue of numbers or the mechanism by which germanicization progressed once Germanic-speaking communities had become established in Britain (see Hines 1998, 160). His work concentrates instead on the Continental origins of various elements of early Anglo-Saxon culture, and their interactions with one another within Britain, a methodology which is not entirely unacceptable to the elite-emulationists (e.g. 1984; 1990 and 1992; a similar approach is also adopted by Böhme 1986).

Returning to the Culture History paradigm, and to the use made of it by scholars studying Germanic-speaking tribal groups in the first millennium AD, we should note that much of the early critique of the paradigm related to the use of the model for identifying ethno-linguistic groups in earlier prehistory. The real target for Clark and the first generation of revisionists were the vast *Kulturkreise* covering large portions of the Continent which gave rise to entirely hypothetical 'ethnic groups' such as the Kurgans and the Beaker People, often identified, on the flimsiest of grounds with the large ethno-linguistic groups observable a millennium or more later such as the Hellenes or the Celts. This approach is not entirely absent from the literature today and there are still those who would seek to link the ethnogenesis of the Germanic language group with the appearance in northern Europe of the "Corded Ware/Battle Axe" culture some two thousand years before the earliest evidence for Germanic speech (e.g. Polomé 1990). This is of course the main thrust of the approach as championed by Kossina (1911) and Childe (1950) but it falls down on a number of methodological grounds. Firstly the assumption of relative immobility from the Late Neolithic or Early Bronze Age, when these large-scale *Kulturkreise* are visible, through to the Late Iron Age when the location of ethnolinguistic groups such as Celts and Germans can first be ascertained seems somewhat incautious. Secondly, in the Late Iron Age, when the territories of the Celtic- and Germanic-speaking tribes can be delimited with some confidence they are notably not linked by unified *Kulturkreise*.

One of the clearest examples of Roman Iron Age Germanic migrations reflected by *Kulturkreise* can be found in the Sîntana de Mures-Černjachov Culture. This cultural grouping has been identified across much of eastern Romania, Moldova and the Ukraine. Extending geographically from the Carpathians to the Don and chronologically from the mid-third to the late-fourth century it would be very difficult to doubt that this *Kulturkreis* reflects the material manifestation of the Gothic settlement which historical sources put in precisely this region for precisely this time period (Heather and Matthews 1991, 54-6). Unlike the Przeworsk Culture of central Germania, attributed to the Vandals, but in a region unfamiliar to Classical authorities, this cultural-grouping lies along the north-eastern frontier of the Roman Empire and even the most critical revisionists would have difficulty in denying its relationship to the Goths. Amongst other distinctive features this cultural grouping displays both *Grubenhäuser* and *Wohnstallhäuser*, house types typical of Germanic Europe in this period but not previously found in these regions (ibid., 57-8). If ever unequivocal archaeological evidence for Germanic migrations was required then it could be found here.

Critics of the Culture History paradigm, operate, like most of the innovators in 'progressive' archaeological theory from the perspective of earlier prehistory when supporting evidence of a non-archaeological kind which they can test their interpretational frameworks against are unavailable and they consequently have a *carte blanche* on which to build their theories and critiques. Those working in the historical periods, however, must not allow themselves to be tyrannized by colleagues working in periods in which the quantity of the data is outweighed by the rhetoric.

Part II

This brief rehearsal of the background to the 'invasion' debate serves to remind us of the failure of dialogue between archaeology, history and philology. To a large extent the insecurities that fired the New Archaeology are ebbing away. Back in the 1960s and '70s single honours archaeology degrees and fully independent archaeology departments were still something of a novelty and practitioners were desperate to prove that they were good for something other than providing the illustrations to history books. Just as now some of us rail against the agenda and interpretative frameworks being set by prehistorians so in the 1960s and before prehistorians were trying to use their data to tell the kind of stories historians had prepared them for; kinds of stories which archaeological data alone is unable to tell convincingly. Unfortunately for us, in the messy divorce which followed Prehistory got custody of Historical Archaeology and a generation grew up trained in the prehistory of the Historical period, so to speak.

Although many of us are aware of the problems this divorce has created there are many factors working against the establishment of a civilised regime of joint custody. Universities' administrative structures, like divorce lawyers, seem to make it difficult for different disciplines to collaborate without bickering over resource allocation and so many good ideas thought up by groups of individuals fail to get institutional backing. At St Andrews, in recent years, a very well thought out Masters programme jointly conceived between the Late Medieval English and Scottish Historians and the Middle English and Middle Scots teachers in the English Department nose-dived, not because the people who would have been teaching the course fell out but because their respective heads of school wanted to micromanage resource allocation to an unfeasible level – each seeing the other as trying to poach his or her FTEs. Some Universities seem much better suited to interdisciplinary projects and I am presently the external examiner for two excellent Masters programmes in Glasgow taught between History, English, Archaeology, Modern Languages and Celtic.

Another problem that hinders interdisciplinary work is that we tend to misuse our sister disciplines through ignorance and that antagonises potential collaborators. What I am thinking about here is the kind of thing which we all do when, writing with great subtly about our own particular field, we allude to how things are done, or what is believed, in another area on the basis of reading one article or a couple of chapters from one book. Even within disciplines we tend to do this chronologically or geographically. The overuse of Evans-Pritchard's ethnography of the Sudan led some people to coin the phrase the 'Nuer' Archaeology. And people, who are fully aware of the debates in their own area, say over early medieval burial practice, will summarise the situation across the channel on the basis of reading a single article on the subject without considering whether or not its author is mainstream, avant-garde, old fashioned or just plain wrong.

I have recently been reading material relating to the British settlement in Armorica. It seems that a fairly large school within Breton archaeology is now arguing, apparently persuasively, that we should date this to the third century rather than the Late Antique period (e.g. Giot, Guigon and Merdrignac 2003). A large part of their case is that northern Gaul was heavily depopulated in this era and thus immigration would have been desirable. This didn't seem to tally with Late Roman historians I had been reading so I asked my brother, Greg Woolf, who is an expert on Roman Gaul. He explained to me that the theory of a third-century depopulation occurred in an accessible and well marketed French-language text-book on Gallo-Roman Archaeology but that it did not represent a consensus view amongst experts working in the field. The author was a likeable elderly academic who had done a lot of good in his time so the younger generation were loathe to confront him directly on this issue. The early medieval Bretonists, finding his book the most accessible, had simply presumed he represented the consensus. To a greater or lesser degree we all do this.

This is partly down to laziness or lack of time but it is also down to aptitude. When we are children or teenagers we don't tend to think of the way that the study of the past is broken down into disciplines. We get interested in the Romans, the Egyptians or the Vikings and read anything we can find on them, usually drawing from a mixture of historical, literary and archaeological primary sources. As we get older and pursue our interests we are forced, generally, to chose a more narrow field and we opt for material culture, historical narrative or languages according to our aptitude. The academic discipline of History stands somewhere in the middle and many social and economic historians share interests with archaeologists whereas others, dealing with the intricacies of complex texts, have more in common with philologists. Philology and Archaeology however, seem a long way apart and I have become convinced that the reason why so many Archaeologists are dismissive of linguistic evidence, and why so many philologists use such crude archaeological paradigms when trying to contextualise their work, is simply because they don't have an aptitude for dealing with those kinds of data. Archaeologists and Philologists find it hard to understand one another because they find it hard to understand one another (*sic*). Two kids who both loved the stories of Ancient Greece and wanted to know the truth about the Trojan War became, respectively, Michael Ventris and Colin Renfrew because of what they were naturally good at. My discipline is not better than yours, I am just better at it that you are, as you are better at yours than I am.

This brings me to the problem of the Archaeological evidence and the Historical evidence not matching up, something we often hear about. Clearly this can never happen. If you believe, as everyone but Michael Shanks does, that there was a real past then all the data we can retrieve from it is a real part of that past. If the History and the Archaeology don't fit it is a problem in the present with the interpretative frameworks.

So how do we move forward? At times, I have to confess, my frustration with post-processualist theory emanating from students of the Neolithic has led me to consider the solution to be the Classics route – that we should have Prehistory Departments and that the archaeology of the historical periods should be taught in History departments, just as a School of Classics or a Department of Ancient History would almost always contain Classical archaeologists. But deep down I know that we would lose more than we would gain by this – as well as the non-period specific technical skills and environmental specialisms, there are grey areas such as Meso-historic periods (that is Dark Ages) and Proto-historic periods (such as the Late pre-Roman Iron Age in Britain and Gaul or Viking Age Scandinavia), and, though I am loathe to admit it, even Neolithic archaeologists occasionally come up with sensible suggestions.

One other approach is to try to stop thinking about the disciplines in monolithic terms. Within Archaeology we are used to thinking of palynologists, pottery specialists and so on; practitioners who have very specific skills. History is the same, and some of these specialisms are in fact remarkably similar to archaeological skills. Let us take two inter-related sub-disciplines that are used to provenance documents and other texts, Palaeography and Diplomatic. These employ essentially typological methodologies.

Palaeography tells us about manuscripts rather than about the texts they contain. It consists, principally of studying letter forms and punctuation conventions and is in principal no different than pottery typology. Indeed one could be a palaeographer without needing to be able to read the language the text was written in and I am fairly certain that any good archaeological typologist, whether of ceramics, lithics or whatever could pick up palaeography very quickly. Like ceramic sequences handwriting styles vary through time and space and tend to follow developmental sequences for which a relative chronology can be fairly easily established. Associated evidence can allow some points in these sequences to be accorded absolute dates, just as with archaeological typology. Indeed since manuscripts are, in fact, artefacts from the past, palaeography *is* an archaeological skill.

Diplomatic also employs a typological methodology and though slightly less secure than palaeography it has the advantage that it can be used to provenance texts rather than just the manuscripts in which they are found. Diplomatic works by typologising the form and layout of the text rather than the handwriting. This may actually include physical layout, the shape the words make on the page, but it can also include formulae. For example before the late 1180s Scottish kings styled themselves, in their Latin charters *Rex Scotiae* – 'King of Scotia', but from about 1188 onwards they adopt the style *Rex Scottorum*. Thus a manuscript purporting to be copy of a charter issued by an earlier king but using the later formula is either a forgery or a less than faithful copy (Broun 2003).

There are within the community of Historians scholars who specialise in these kinds of typological study just as there are such people within the archaeological field. If we try and think of each other as specialists in a wide range of specific fields, more or less different from one another, rather than as two tribes then we may find it easier to find common ground and to call upon each other rather than compete for possession of the past.

Conclusion

Philology is likewise a typological science and historical linguistics works in exactly the same way as palaeography or ceramic analysis (or indeed the identification of skeletal remains). Languages, in part and as whole systems, can be analysed typologically and arranged in typological sequences. In contemporary discourse about the past, however, philology has become very much the poor relation. Few universities create opportunities to study the subject at an introductory level and the scholarly discourse is often set at a very high level. Before the Second World War, however, it played a key role in shaping historical and archaeological debates and we work in the shadow of that era. Although few historians or archaeologists show much interest in the evidence language can provide for social and cultural development those of us working on early mediaeval material still, overwhelmingly, divide into sub-disciplines on the basis of the language spoken by our subjects. The Anglo-Saxons were Anglo-Saxons because they spoke English (everything else, DNA or material culture, is secondary to this), and this is what fundamentally separated them from the Britons with whom they cohabited. For the most part modern scholars working on the early medieval period in the British Isles work principally on the English or the Celtic-speaking peoples. It is also notable that Anglo-Saxonists are more likely to have the Scandinavians (another linguistically-defined group) as a second string to their bow than any Celtic-speaking group. This reflects the philologically determined agendas of the nineteenth and early twentieth century. This divide in scholarship is so marked that I have been able to make a career by straddling the Celtic/Germanic divide, a feat which so impresses people in itself that I don't have to be an expert in either field.

In 1972 Thomas Charles-Edwards wrote that:

> The disintegration of a single language into a group of languages is an effect of the disintegration of a society. Language mirrors society. Not only do languages contain systems of social classification and description, changes in whole languages are part of the process by which societies change. So much is evident that the existence of a single society requires linguistic communication between its members (Charles-Edwards 1972, 4).

Such a view is not now popular although it seems to me to be a self-evident truth. In the modern world a shared language allows for employment mobility and supportive social networking. I suspect that the fact that in the modern world people can learn languages in a class, from tapes or through a 'teach yourself' book has rather distracted people from the fact that before the last century most people were only able to learn languages well through long term association with native speakers. In the Late Roman Republic all the aristocrats were bilingual in Greek because their parents had bought educated Greek slaves to teach them. In the imperial period this bilingualism became increasingly less common in part at least because educated Greeks were now fully incorporated within the Empire and ceased to become available for slavery.

In the early Middle Ages the casual acquisition of language was not really an option. Languages were passed on through sustained intimacy and transformed in the same way. Any model for the spread of Englishness must take this fact on board (Woolf 2007). Given this, however, the only data which will allow us to explore sustained intimacy would seem to be settlement archaeology. We need to examine social distance both within settlements and between settlements. If we imagine, as seems likely, that the Anglo-Saxons derived their biological inheritance from both Germanic invaders and Romano-British natives we have to develop models which explain how individual Britons could be absorbed into English communities without bringing too much linguistic baggage with them. The evidence of Philology combined with DNA tells us that this happened, but only archaeology has a chance of telling how it happened.

Bibliography

Primary sources:

DBG = Edwards, H.J., 1917, ed. & tr. Julius Caesar, *De Bello Gallico*, Loeb Classical Library v.72, Harvard University Press (London)

Secondary sources:

Anthony, D.W. 1990. 'Migration in archaeology: the baby and the bathwater', *American Anthropologist*, 92: 895-914

Arnold, C.J. 1984. *Roman Britain to Saxon England*, Croom Helm (London)

Böhme, H. 1986. 'Das ende der Römerherrschaft in Britannien und die angelsächsische besiedlung Englands im 5. jahrhundert', *Jahrbuch des Römisch-Germanisch Zentralmuseums, Mainz*, 33: 469-574

Broun, D. 2003. 'The absence of regnal years from the dating clause of the charters of the kings of Scots,' *Anglo-Norman Studies*, 25: 47-63

Chadwick, J. and Ventris, M. 1956. *Documents in Mycenaean Greek: Three Hundred Selected Tablets From Knossos, Pylos, and Mycenae with Commentary and Vocabulary*, Cambridge University Press (Cambridge)

Champion, T. 1990. 'Migration revived', *Journal of Danish Archaeology*, 9: 214-218

Charles-Edwards, T.M. 1972. 'Kinship, status and the origins of the Hide', *Past and Present*, 56: 5-35

Childe, V.G. 1950. *Prehistoric Migrations in Europe*, Harvard University Press (Cambridge, Mass.)

Clark, G. 1966. 'The invasion hypothesis in British archaeology', *Antiquity*, 40: 172-89

Cunliffe, B. 1995. *Iron Age Britain*, Batsford (London)

Giot, P.-R., Guigon, P. and Merdrignac, B. 2003. *The British Settlement of Brittany: the First Bretons in Armorica*, Tempus (Stroud)

Hamerow, H. 1994. 'Migration theory and the Migration Period', in B. Vyner (ed.), *Building on the Past: Papers Celebrating 150 years of the Royal Archaeological Institute*, Royal Archaeological Institute (London): 164-77

Hawkes, C.F.C. 1959. 'The A B C of the British Iron Age', *Antiquity*, 33: 170-182

Heather, P. and Matthews, J. 1991. *The Goths in the Fourth Century*, Liverpool University Press (Liverpool)

Higham, N.J. 1992. *Rome, Britain and the Anglo-Saxons*, Seaby (London)

Hines, J. 1984. *The Scandinavian Character of Anglian England in the Pre-Viking Period*, B.A.R., British Series, 124 (Oxford)

Hines, J. 1990. 'Philology, archaeology and the *adventus Saxonum vel Anglorum*', in A. Bammesberger and A. Wollman (ed.), *Britain 400-600: Language and History*, Winter (Heidelberg): 17-36

Hines, J. 1992. 'The Scandinavian character of Anglian England: an update', in M.O.H. Carver (ed.), *The Age of Sutton Hoo: the Seventh Century in North Western Europe*, Boydell (Woodbridge): 315-29

Hines, J. 1998. 'The Anglian migration in British historical research', *Studien zur Sachsenforschung*, 11: 155-166

Hodges, R. 1989. *The Anglo-Saxon Achievement*, Duckworth (London)

Kossina, G. 1911. *Die Herkunft der Germanen: Zur Methode der Siedlungsarchäologie*, Kabitzsch (Würzburg)

Kristiansen, K. 1991. 'Prehistoric migrations: the case of the Single Grave and Corded Ware Cultures', *Journal of Danish Archaeology*, 8: 211-225

Polomé, E. 1990. 'Linguistic paleontology: migration theory, prehistory, and archaeology correlated with linguistic data', in E. Polomé (ed.), *Research Guide on Language Change*, Trends in Linguistics; studies and monographs, 48, Mouton de Gruyter (Berlin): 137-159

Renfrew, C. 1969. 'Trade and culture process in European Prehistory', *Current Anthropology*, 10: 151-169

Renfrew, C. 1979. 'Systems collapse as social transformation: catastrophe and anastrophe in early state societies', in K.L. Cooke and C. Renfrew (eds.), *Transformations: Mathematical Approaches to Culture Change*, Academic Press (London): 481-506

Renfrew, C. 1982. 'Post-collapse resurgence: culture process in the Dark Ages', in C. Renfrew and S. Shennan (eds.), *Ranking, Resources and Exchange*, Cambridge University Press (Cambridge): 113-116

Renfrew, C. 1987. *Archaeology and Language: the Puzzle of Indo-European Origins*, Cape (London)

Welch, M. 1985. 'Rural settlement patterns in the Early and Middle Anglo-Saxon period', *Landscape History*, 7: 13-25

Welch, M. 1992. *Anglo-Saxon England*, Batsford (London)

Woolf, A. 2007. 'Apartheid and economics in Anglo-Saxon England', in N. Higham (ed.), *The Britons in Anglo-Saxon England*, Boydell (Woodbridge): 115-129

The practical implications of interdisciplinary approaches: research in Anglo-Saxon East Anglia

Morn Capper

Interdisciplinary history makes use of the concepts, theory, or evidence of other disciplines; as such it has developed no unifying corpus of methodology or theory of its own. Yet the call for interdisciplinarity has become embedded as a matter of practice in medieval studies, particularly in the relationship between History and Archaeology. As the need for an awareness of the findings of other disciplines and for the uses of interdisciplinary practice in studying the medieval period have become more institutionalised, there is a need for the practitioner to consider what assumptions are being made and how these are dealt with. This article represents the reworking of a discussion paper framed from reflective analysis to raise practical and open-ended questions for discussion, particularly regarding the role of interdisciplinarity in the current context of University based research.

At a conference entitled 'Approaching Interdisciplinarity' it is very pertinent to question what interdisciplinarity is and what it can be made to do. For me, interdisciplinarity relates to the analytical interaction between the evidence types produced by different disciplines. The question is whether the interdisciplinary analysis that is undertaken produces results which are only the sum of the knowledge of constituent disciplines, or whether the results produced are more than the sum. Can the same piece of material culture or data set be analysed differently in a multi-disciplinary context? Can different or additional questions be developed for an interdisciplinary corpus of evidence, amplifying the potential level of understanding? As the practitioner increases the breadth of evidence to be analysed in any finite project, it is inevitable that the scope of the project will decrease accordingly elsewhere, for example in chronological or geographical range. It is important in justifying an interdisciplinary approach that the potential synergy of the multiple evidence types will add depth in analysis and give new insight to the project. This paper will consider the background of interdisciplinarity and the potentials and pitfalls of interdisciplinary analysis. Through critical reflection, the benefits and difficulties of interdisciplinarity for the practitioner during postgraduate research will act as a platform for wider questions regarding the role and practical implications of interdisciplinarity and why it is still an important practical consideration in current medieval research.

The background of interdisciplinarity between History and Archaeology

There has been an interest in interdisciplinary collaboration between Archaeology and History in the medieval period since the early years of the *Annales* 'School', due particularly to Marc Bloch's *La Société Féodale* from 1939-1940 (Bloch 1954; Bloch 1961). To give the influence of *Annales* due consideration here would take a further paper in itself (Burke 1990). Looking at more recent reasons behind interest in interdisciplinarity, the application of pertinent theories from other relevant disciplines was a feature of the drive toward a scientific professionalism in both disciplines during the '60s and '70s – particular examples being the application of literary theory in the case of history and the application of geographical spatial modelling in the case of archaeology. The relationship between History and Archaeology was profoundly affected by their common interest in the use of anthropological models to add depth to explanations of pre-Modern societies, for example the influence of the work of anthropologist Evans Pritchard on witchcraft in Azande on both disciplines, as in the discussions of Early Modern witchcraft by Keith Thomas (Evans Pritchard 1937; Thomas 1970; Thomas 1971). Thomas advocated the value of anthropological models for discussions of key topics of specific interest to medievalists: myth, genealogy, kingship, bloodfeud and kinship (Thomas 1963, 9-14). The most ardent early exponent of practical interdisciplinary borrowing by archaeologists from cultural anthropological approaches came from the archaeologist Lewis Binford, and anthropology has been a constant feature in archaeological thought ever since (Binford 1962; Trigger 2006). Natalie Zieman Davies commented on the four features of anthropological work which could be useful to the Historian: '...close observation of living processes of social interaction; interesting ways of interpreting symbolic behaviour; suggestions about how the parts of a social system fit together; and material from cultures very different from those which historians are used to studying' (Zieman Davis 1981, 267). The works of anthropologist Jack Goody were key influences of the 'linguistic turn' in History, discussing orality and the method and importance of the advent of writing. These discussions were important to Clanchy's (1970) discussion of law and memory 'Remembering the past and the good old law' and to his (1979) work on the central middle ages *From Memory to Written Record*. Clanchy's studies negotiated the transfer of anthropological concepts without the 'technological determinism', translating the terminology and constructs for the medieval period (McKitterick 1990, 4-5). Goody's work was also of great interest to archaeologists studying historical periods, such as Colin Renfrew (Renfrew 1980, 297). Common interest of archaeology and history in anthropological models and theories, has led in recent years to common questions, resulting in the formulation of complementary research questions. This has particularly been the case in the realms of cultural history and historical archaeology.

As has often been rehearsed, at first the potential for collaboration between Archaeology and History was not always welcomed, and this was also true for the medieval period. In 1979 Eric Hobsbawm expressed that the role of Archaeology was to be part of History (Hobsbawm 1979, 249). David Austin blamed the historical agenda for the divisions between historic and prehistoric archaeology, stating 'we medieval archaeologists have jeopardized our negotiation with prehistory and alienated ourselves from the developing archaeological agenda' and even advocated the abandonment of the integration of material culture with the historical record (Austin 1990, 13). Timothy Champion famously wrote of 'the tyranny of the historical record' (Champion 1990, 79). The propensity for interdisciplinary history in general and in the medieval period in particular has also often depended on the disciplinary context of History and Archaeology within academia in different countries (Jordanova 2000, 87-9; Reuter 2006, 7). However, the rise of post-modernist views of history, and alongside them archaeological post-processualism including the move towards interpretive archaeology (e.g. Tilley 1993), has allowed for a parallel understanding of texts and material culture as performing a similar role in society. Ian Hodder's ideas of contextual archaeology require that material culture is interpreted not only according to general symbolic principles or tendencies, but also the ways in which these are re-arranged as part of strategies of individuals and groups in a particular context, creating a whole that is particular, i.e. dependent on context (Hodder 1982, 217). Hodder has asserted that historical texts are a part of material culture and argued that 'archaeology should recapture its traditional links with history (Hodder 1986, 77).

A common interest in anthropological theory and approaches has served as a third-party mediator in communications when studying the early medieval period in particular, and for thinking about objects and texts in the same ways. For example historian Patrick Geary has interpreted the circulation of medieval relics as material remains according to anthropological models of exchange – interpreting relics as commodities, in an unusual category of 'objects that are both persons and things', a category also applied to slaves by anthropologist Igor Kopytoff in the same volume (Geary 1986, 169; Kopytoff 1986). John Moreland has made important contributions to ideas on the significance of literacy and of writing as a technology of power, analysing the interaction between documents and archaeological sources (Moreland 2001, 83-4). However, at times even the early medieval period has still provided a very good example of how historians and archaeologists fail to interact (Halsall 1997, 817). Interest in theoretical borrowing may fail to include adequate understanding of criticisms raised in anthropological debate – in the case of Clifford Geertz it has been suggested that historians had 'made the cardinal sin of following an anthropologist, not anthropologists and certainly not anthropology' (Goodman 1997, 784-9).[1]

Access to the outside influence of theory from the Social Sciences has been important in the current r'approchement of the two disciplines, working on themes such as identity. However, the work of thinkers such as Walter Goffart (1988) suggests that current views of historical texts themselves as literary constructs may yet draw the historian away from the need to model views of the medieval world on observable human societies. As post-modern debates on issues such as ethnicity burn themselves out, is it true that early medieval historians are left in what one archaeologist has described as a 'theoretical malaise' when trying to actively consider the past (Curta 2007, 165)? In a potentially confusing world where the past is a text and texts are read as artefacts (Spiegel 1997), their contents interpreted through 'archaeology' (Dumville 1987), and where material culture can be viewed as a text (Tilley 1991), is there a need to consider more actively the need to define interdisciplinarity in the medieval period in theory and practice? One has to question whether new theoretical interests will also serve interdisciplinary thinking in the same way, and ask if the disciplines of Archaeology and History will continue to ask parallel questions in the medieval period should common interest in certain types of theoretical issues abate.

Practical concerns over interdisciplinary approaches?

Exponents in the arena of medieval studies are often at the forefront in advocating interdisciplinary analysis. The journals of the early medieval period in particular – *Early Medieval Europe, Anglo-Saxon England, Anglo-Saxon Studies in Archaeology and History* – specify a commitment in their editorial policies to interdisciplinarity. Most early medievalists would advocate the importance of interdisciplinary awareness in the period, whether or not they are engaging in interdisciplinary practice themselves. However, all too often the use of evidence from other disciplines will consist of using select examples or material culture as illustrative, based on questions prompted by the historical record, or vice versa by a historical parallel analysis which does not consider fully the variety or variable reliability of written sources or is limited to documents in translation (Halsall 1997, 817-21). Arguably to do this may be acceptable for an historian or archaeologist who does not claim to work in an interdisciplinary way, producing a separate dialogue, but for the medievalist to do this may introduce such evidence in a subordinate role, obscure the research context, or limit the historian's understanding of the significance of the data. Even where the records produced by other disciplines are considered in a fashion which suggests that equal validity is being given, and the evidence is being considered in genuine concert, the ontological processes inherent in authoritative communication within the framework of an

---

[1] In short, the anthropological works, which continue to influence both archaeology and history, are themselves being constantly challenged and re-assessed (Jordanova 1992). Anthropologists and archaeologists may also be more willing to acknowledge the conflicts inherent in using living cultures for these purposes (Layton 1989).

audience in one's own discipline tend to prioritise the disciplinary agenda and subordinate other material. Whether such use of evidence between disciplines can be effective has remained a topic of debate.

Recently there has been an increased recognition that some periods, the study of the Viking Age in particular, require collaborative interdisciplinary working. The necessity for this is clearly set out by Dawn Hadley and Julian D. Richards, in that exponents of different disciplines working in isolation 'have failed to realize or account for the incompatibilities that exist' (Hadley and Richards 2000, 13). However, the comprehension of 'interdisciplinary' working as a collaborative act has detracted from the fact that medievalists of various disciplines integrate different evidence types on an almost daily basis. As an example of a historical topic which could also be tackled using an interdisciplinary perspective, in an interesting recent article on topographies of memory a historian considers how in monastic legends the ordering of space can be considered through the evidence of 'charters, royal diplomas, hagiography, reliquaries, sculpture and even architectural design' (Remensnyder 2002, 195); such an approach might gain much from the parallel analysis of the spatial distribution of archaeological remains. However, the effectiveness of interdisciplinarity in projects by individuals remains contentious. In a review of several recent monographs from the early medieval period, Catherine Hills has questioned the use made of archaeological evidence by historians, several times describing it as 'misleading', raising as part of her criticisms the persistent question of communication between historians and archaeologists (Hills 2007, 194).[2] Medieval evidence is usually read in knowing reference to the dominant narratives produced by the various disciplines involved, thus the potential to maintain truly separate disciplinary perspectives appears small. As individuals are likely to interrogate evidence about which a dialogue has been produced in other disciplines, it seems to me advisable to acknowledge and reflect on the cross-pollination which occurs between disciplinary narratives during interpretation. The debate on the methodology by which disciplines interact is a constant reminder of the importance of being reflective regarding our practices.

If medievalists think outside disciplinary boundaries on a daily basis, are eclectic in their use of theory, and often may have more interests in common with each other than with other parts of our own disciplines, are we witnessing the demise of medieval disciplinarity? The answer is clearly not. Trained as a dual honours student reading archaeology and history, it may be that I had presumed the possibility that by having a foot in both disciplines I could over-ride the divisions between them. Ten years later I have a very different perspective. I suspect that the importance of professionalism and disciplinarity in defining the methodology of study for texts and material culture is above all formative in the bodies of material produced. The disciplinary context of heritage protection and museum display (Karp and Lavine 1991), planning legislation such as PPG16 and developer funding are important influences on the research agendas of modern archaeological excavation (see discussions in Darvill and Russell 2002; also at www.[1], www.[2]). The excavation of a site is a question-led exercise, as is the selection of historical sources. There is real variability between regions in numismatics – within institutional structures, where it may be linked with archaeology, and in the relationships between museums and metal detectorists – influenced in part by the precious metal content of coins, which puts most medieval coinage under *The Treasure Act* 1996 (www.[3]). In the modern academic context, issues including the role of external partner agencies and funding bodies must be understood as well as the differential survival of manuscripts between regions by the medieval historian who asks why some research questions are more difficult to answer than others. It seems probable that interdisciplinarity cannot and maybe should not be used to try to avoid disciplinary constructs – the effect of disciplinarity in forming the methodology by which texts, sites and material culture are analysed means that analysis of the early medieval period can be interdisciplinary but never really extra-disciplinary. The data and texts under analysis, the context of preservation, the metaphors, parallel examples and terminology in which analysis is located, have been produced by and must be understood within the disciplinary framework of their production. Likewise all researchers must decide to make their academic contributions from one context or the other.

Collaborative and individual potential

It seems that defining how interdisciplinarity aids medieval studies may be clearer in theoretical approaches than in the practical considerations of skills and use of evidence in a research context. All of the above issues create a genuine dilemma for practitioners within medieval studies as to the practicability of interdisciplinary analysis, which will be carried out on one of two models: on a collaborative or individual basis. It is important to consider the benefits and difficulties in collaborative research to assess why individual research may at times be more practical; some ideas for individual practice will be clarified further below, based on reflections from my experience of recent interdisciplinary projects.

An important justification for collaborative interdisciplinary research depends on combining the skills and knowledge of practitioners. In 2000 Dawn Hadley and Julian D. Richards acknowledged the

---

[2] Although this article had not yet appeared at the time this paper was first given, it has been constructive for this discussion to refer to it here. Even more recently in his editorial for *Antiquity*, Martin Carver (2007) commented on a conference held at Oxford to celebrate 50 years of the journal *Medieval Archaeology*, suggesting that 'historical explanation sits in the chair, while archaeological theory occupies the foot-stool'. It seems important to recognise that the debate on the practice of medieval archaeology and with it the distinctiveness of historical archaeology within the discipline is more alive than we might like to admit.

problems caused in Viking studies by the need for such a depth of knowledge that '[i]ndividual scholars cannot hope to embrace the full range of evidence' (Hadley and Richards 2000, 13). In an ideal context it might be assumed that collaboration would solve these problems. However, it is also the case that medieval studies institutions and departments pride themselves on the ability to support interdisciplinary research topics, and that individual interdisciplinary research approaches must be viable. Those individuals who do practice interdisciplinarity on a regular basis tend to have an exceptional breadth of knowledge accrued over time (I am thinking here of scholars such as Chris Wickham or Brian Ward Perkins) and to structure broad studies in such a way as to focus the narrative on key examples or themes rather than a general synthesis; for example Chris Wickham's (2005) *Framing the Early Middle Ages* puts important focus on the comparative analysis of the control of land and trade as key factors in economic and political developments across the European continent, but deals less with religion and culture. This can be a necessary part of the process of making such a project manageable. It is also certainly true that at times the interdisciplinary practitioner will have to accept the authority of experts in other fields. However, collaborative approaches, whilst common in the sciences, do bring their own problems, one might suggest for example:

- the necessity for agreement in group formation, both in terms of individuals and partner agencies, and in the formulation of research questions.
- project ownership and authority between the collaborating persons and institutions, in particular relative credit given between collaborators of different status: academics, PhD students and non-PhD collaborators (Endersby 1996; Heffner 1979; Zuckerman 1968).
- commitment and project funding, particularly in the context of current resource discrepancies between arts and sciences.
- questions of preferred arenas of publication (though there are an increasing number of medieval publications which acknowledge interdisciplinary perspectives).[3]
- The possibility of levels of compromise in the academic basis and interpretation of findings that some practitioners may find unacceptable.

There can be no doubt that collaborative interdisciplinary projects have enormous potential. Collaborative series such as *The Transformation of the Roman World* and *Studies in Archaeoethnology*, often the product of meetings of scholars, have had a groundbreaking influence on some topics. However, it is necessary to consider that through the specialisation or scope of research individual medievalists may choose to engage in interdisciplinary analysis. Such projects are currently underway at many British institutions. The following reflective points of practice may be of interest in questioning ways in which interdisciplinarity can impact on the development of both the researcher and research project.

Individual interdisciplinarity – project planning and research

I have come to reflect on the question of interdisciplinarity through two research projects investigating history and identity within Anglo-Saxon kingdoms using historical sources, archaeology and numismatics. The first project was a study to resolve the conflicting narratives given by these disciplines for consideration of the East Anglian kingdom from c.700 to c.950; as an independent kingdom, as part of the Mercian polity and as part of West Saxon conquests of the early tenth century (Capper 2003). This project challenged the perceived orthodoxy that from the seventh century onwards East Anglia was effectively a client kingdom of its more powerful neighbours, its rulers 'scarcely of note' and capable of realising only brief periods of independence before falling, inevitably, to the Scandinavian invaders (Stenton 1971, 51-3; Higham 1999, 155).[4] This project investigated how aspects of regional written and material culture, for example material artefacts, economic ties and religious cults, reflect multiple identities, and how they were used in accommodation to negotiate the acceptance or resistance of outside identities at a regional level. More recently my doctoral thesis *Contested loyalties, regional and national identities in the midland kingdoms of Anglo-Saxon England, c.700-c.900* (Capper 2008) uses an interdisciplinary approach to re-examine the development of identities in the midlands and their interaction as part of relations of power along ethnic, religious and political lines. This research focuses on the relationship between regional subkingdoms within the expanding Mercian polity between the seventh and ninth centuries, and questions how identity and interaction in the Anglo-Saxon kingdoms was influenced by their constituent peoples and by local and regional interest. It also considers links between the Mercian hegemony and its insular and continental neighbours, and assesses how the cultural links of subordinated peoples, both to each other and to continental kingdoms, were changed by processes of subjugation. Both projects have led me to question the ways in which bodies of evidence, and the disciplinary constructs within which they are investigated, interact during the process of analysis.

---

[3] The issues of interdisciplinary publication have been discussed by Germano (1999). Journals still tend to be divided along disciplinary lines, although the important series *Anglo-Saxon Studies in Archaeology and History* demonstrates the benefits of an integrated approach.

[4] This project was completed prior to the publication of Tim Pestell's (2004) book on the monastic landscape in Anglo-Saxon East Anglia, with which it overlaps at points and I generally agree with many of Tim's conclusions.

Skills and knowledge

Any analysis of an interdisciplinary study must begin by questioning its practicability. A significant gap between disciplines is the different skill base needed to understand and properly analyse the different evidence types. Even if one has training in historical and archaeological methods, during the course of graduate research the practitioner faces a constant need to expand their research capabilities: whether in terms of background knowledge, or in languages or I.T. skills necessary to evaluate the evidence and the surrounding debate. However, whilst research methods and perspectives will be part of any postgraduate research training, the decision to undertake an interdisciplinary study can be influential in refocusing further research time into training, a decision which may also impact on project supervision. The need to understand historical evidence will involve more specific training in historical skills and languages (Jordanova 2000, 179-80) – Medieval Latin, archival skills and paleography for the medievalist, probably also regional languages such as Old English or Old Norse. Due to the variety of evidence types there may be some skills from other disciplines that are not available through the framework of a taught degree or research programme and may have to be self-taught, or acquired through external training or knowledge exchange with peers, for example additional information on palaeography or material culture, codicology, runic inscriptions or numismatics.

In considering the case of Anglo-Saxon East Anglia, the regional prevalence of numismatic data may be surprising to those unfamiliar with the archaeological context of the region. The role of coinage as evidence in archaeological investigation, particularly in its practical role as a tool of archaeological dating is well known (Archibald 1988). It may be helpful here to include a reminder of the value of coinage to the medieval historian, helpfully summarised by Henry Loyn as follows:

> '...superb historical evidence in little space, at their best with the name of the king in whose name they were struck, the mint at which they were struck, the name of the moneyer with immediate responsibility for striking. Equally powerfully they give insight into the economy that used them, yielding vital information on weight, degree of fineness, artistry, and also (with the help of sophisticated statistical techniques) some measure of the volume of the separate issues' (Loyn 1991, 29).

Possibly based in part on questions of professionalism within the discipline itself, as well as the base of many numismatists within museums rather than academic departments, very few medieval departments appear to undertake any kind of active training in numismatic procedures or methods. Many practitioners in Archaeology or History may not be fully aware of the basic conflicts between historical and numismatic paradigms, for example in the East Anglian kingdom as will be discussed below. All researchers will rely at times on the generosity of other members of the academic community, but the importance of investigating the discipline-specific skills base through which evidence has been analysed is particularly vital and particularly time consuming to the interdisciplinary practitioner if they intend to conduct their discussion with any authority.

Establishing a research context

A common problem in interdisciplinary study is one of precedent. Due to a lack of precedent for this type of study in my first project on East Anglia, the preliminary identification and selection of an interdisciplinary source base took longer than originally anticipated. The fragmentary and diverse nature of the sources generated the need for a much greater level of background reading than would otherwise have been necessary. The university structures within which research is undertaken can significantly affect the facility with which material can be assembled, but also the research environment within which it is engaged. Those medievalists engaged within disciplinary departments must build networks to avoid being isolated from medievalists working in other fields, those in medieval studies departments risk being isolated from cross-period discussions at the forefront of key theoretical concepts within their own disciplines – traditional bodies of theory such as gender, but also more recent trends such as subaltern studies, concepts of time and victimhood. Disciplinary practices also influence the availability of unpublished material, not only PhD dissertations, but particularly the context of forthcoming materials and most importantly in the grey literature.[5] In archaeology in particular there was and is a 'research gap', in which delays in the appearance of published work and the difficulties in locating and accessing grey literature resources may be a barrier to effective synthesis of results even within the discipline itself (see Falkingham 2005; www.[5]). Numismatic evidence may cause particular problems, as much of the most useful evidence is discussed in different arenas over time: more select journals, internal museum publications, in records of nineteenth-century antiquarian discoveries and now in online metal detecting discussion forums. The collation of additional materials – reports on sources, background reading and an extensive bibliography – was a worthwhile but time consuming necessity in formulating a research area, which quickly demonstrated the

---

[5] Grey literature can be broadly defined for these purposes as non-commercial publications produced by government, academia, business and industry, published by them, by the alternative press or over the Internet, in print or in electronic formats. Some pertinent examples would include theses and unpublished papers, but also newsletters, internal reports for business development or reports to government or planning bodies to meet legislative criteria such as PPG16. For some background on the definition of such material see Coonin (2003). This literature can have a more immediate and sometimes greater role in driving research agendas within disciplines than published material, and raise additional complementary or conflicting research questions, but may not be freely available or widely known beyond the discipline itself. Since the advent of the Internet such literature has become more widely available, but much harder to define, with wider debate on the definition of grey literature, its impact on research, its authenticity and authority behind its content. See Weintraub (2000) and www[4].

importance of appreciating how the disciplinary context of method and audience had been formative in shaping the corpus of evidence available to the researcher.

Methodology and research questions

The preliminary analysis of interdisciplinary background reading made it evident that the various disciplines presented conflicting paradigms for the Anglo-Saxon Kingdoms, in this case for the history of Middle Saxon East Anglia. The interdisciplinary context was therefore fundamental in the formulation of a research question. The central proposal for an MA study was to use interdisciplinary analysis to assess the role of the Anglo-Saxon kingdom of East Anglia in the period in which written sources only allowed an external perspective, between the death of Aelfwald in 749 and the mid-tenth century. The aim of this study was twofold:

i) To attempt to establish a chronology for events within East Anglia, by reconciling the conflicting paradigms derived from the evidence of the different disciplines.
ii) To provide an East Anglian perspective on the events of the Mercian supremacy, the Viking invasions and the expansion of Wessex, and to attempt to situate the East Anglian kingdom in the context of these events.

The most significant development was the determination that sources for Middle Saxon East Anglia could not be genuinely considered in concert due to the fragmentary body of evidence, which left little overlap and so little room to draw comparisons between bodies of evidence. This led to the formulation of a new research methodology to enable the complementary analysis of the material and textual evidence as I have discussed elsewhere (Capper 2005).[6]

The writing up of an interdisciplinary study may be problematic. In this case, the presentation of the study to an audience suitable for a History project required the explanation of the theoretical and practical aspects of the use of each of the other types of evidence. This included the different measurements, dating methods, scientific analysis types and analysis of their limitations, stylistic criteria, and so on for each discipline. It was also necessary to highlight the significance and reliability of the variations between pieces of evidence to a much greater degree for an audience essentially unfamiliar with this type of data. This additional material, where possible, was presented in footnotes as well as appendices to demonstrate stylistic variations in coinage and archaeological artefacts. However, the need to clarify the context of each piece of evidence also interfered significantly with the flow of the analysis in places.

Scope and timescales

Despite the careful selection of evidence, the more extensive discussion and justification of the various sources produced an excess of equally relevant data necessary to the construction of the final analysis. The need to establish the chronology for the kingdom and to reconcile the hypotheses proposed by the various disciplines before proceeding to my own analysis of the evidence was the most useful, but also the most problematic part of the study. In tackling the paradigms presented by writers from different disciplines a genuinely interdisciplinary analysis could be reached and original perspectives on important past processes achieved. However, the need to tackle a wider body of existing theories combined with the excess of relevant data worked to over-extend the research phase and the length of the discussion. With hindsight, it would have been relatively easy to restrict and streamline the topic chronologically during earlier phases, but this might have led to incomplete resolution of the research question. Streamlining undertaken during the process of writing up may struggle to avoid affecting the coherence of the project and give an inaccurate impression in places that the material has been dealt with in a cursory fashion. A significant problem of interdisciplinary methodology is therefore that the wider scope of the potential evidence for a project restricts the chronological or geographical potential of a study, and may extend the timeframe. This in some ways justifies the perception of cross-disciplinary collaboration as a more suitable methodology for tackling such a project, provided that suitable partners can be found and possibly also the extension of the doctoral timetable.

Suggestions for development in interdisciplinary methodology

The pursuit of interdisciplinary questions during this study and subsequently has led me to question whether as individual practitioners in the medieval period we are always aware of the extent to which disciplinary constructs frame our research and how interdisciplinary evidence fits into this framework? This has led me, at this early stage in my career, to make some suggestions on the following broader research issues which impact on the interdisciplinary relationships promoted in the medieval period.

---

[6] The basis of this work was the conjunction of the specific circumstances of Anglo-Saxon East Anglia with the work of Mark Leone (1988) on the eighteenth-century gardens of Annapolis, wherein a historical text was used as an independent framework. Leone argued that the use of one evidence type to assess another was valid because the artefacts and written records could be seen as independent and non-identical phenomena. As both the material and written records are produced by the activities of the same society I would find it difficult to accept this suggestion for the Middle Ages in general. However, in the case of East Anglia from *c.*749 to the mid-tenth century, the information preserved in the written records concerning the East Anglian kingdom is either temporally or spatially dislocated, if not both. All surviving contemporary records such as the *Anglo-Saxon Chronicle* are produced outside the kingdom, whilst the records from within the kingdom are much later, written by elites formed after the West Saxon conquest of the Danish Kingdom. Thus, unusually, the separate production of the archaeological and the surviving written records can be asserted.

Chronology and periodisation

'All periodisation is artifice, but it is not arbitrary' (Nelson 2002, 15).

The delineation of periods and the impact of choosing to establish a chronology, for example of key events, is a process of selection and prioritisation. As such these processes have an effect on historical analysis which is not always recognised (see Foot 2005). It has at times been argued that the medieval period itself is a construct which has the potential to limit dialogue (Reuter 1998, 25). If the Vikings are no longer the *deus ex machina* force of ninth-century Europe, is it too soon to get rid of 'The Viking Age'? (Hodges 2006, 157). H. E. Carr said that '[t]he division of history into periods is not a fact, but a necessary hypothesis or a tool of thought, valid in so far as it is illuminating, and dependent for its validity on interpretation (Carr 1961, 54-55). In archaeology in 1995 Hodder suggested that 'the definition and dating of chronological phases ...are fundamental to most if not all archaeological endeavour...but there has been little theory...' (Hodder 1995, 164). Citing the influence of Paul Ricoeur, that events possess the same structure as narratives and that therefore their narrative representations can be regarded as explanations of them, Hodder argued that 'the sequence of material culture changes is constituted via narrative content of the material culture' and so 'the stories people live by are not only conscious in their minds, but also concern wider consequences' (Hodder 1995, 168). Therefore the periodisation of the past via sequences of material culture is just as appropriate and at the same time as interpretative as the historical method of periodisation by significant events or phases of activity. As an example, the periodisation of the history of East Anglia, either through the historian's externally determined chronology of key events or processes such as 'The Mercian Supremacy' or 'The First Viking Age' or by the archaeologist's external imposition of the 'Early', 'Middle' and 'Late' Saxon periods, represents the use of tools of analysis – as neither framework particularly reflects an internal chronology of the kingdom, the project observed the relevance of, but was not defined by, these boundaries.[7]

In this context, choice of chronology presents the interdisciplinary researcher with a dilemma, as it should be understood that the way in which historical and archaeological records fit into a timeframe can be very different. The attempt to integrate the historical record, which tends to privilege events, and the archaeological record, which tends to privilege processes can be an inexact tool. In the early medieval period the chronology of historical sources tends to be framed in very precise terms, via annals based on Easter Tables or from the dating of charters through one or more methods which may not agree, by regnal year, incarnation year (AD dating) indiction and so forth (Fryde 1986; Hines, Høilund, Neilsen and Siegmund 1999; Poole 1921). The relative chronology provided by sites may be pinned if one is lucky by relatively specific dendrochronology dating, by a range of dates as given by radiocarbon dating, or by reference to other processes which are much broader still. Two examples of important developments in the archaeological record relating to the consideration of Anglo-Saxon East Anglia are Susan Oosthuizen's (2005) identification of the laying out of the Middle Saxon field system at Bourn Brooke near Cambridge, or the expansion of Ipswich ware distribution during the eighth century as analysed by Keith Wade in response to Paul Blinkhorn's as yet unpublished Ipswich ware project (Wade 2001; Blinkhorn forthcoming). Both processes have been linked to the expanding power of the Mercian supremacy, yet absolute dating is impossible. Attempts to refine archaeological dating through processes such as Bayesian analysis have been constructive in highlighting the divergence between chronologies produced by radiocarbon dating and other contextual dating methods, such as coinage, as used for example by Chris Scull in discussing the expansion of the trading settlement at Ipswich in the seventh and eighth centuries (Scull and Bayliss 1999). However, the refining of scientific archaeological dating using an interpretative framework of finds must be applied carefully, to avoid the danger of the paradigm reproducing itself.

The integration of numismatic chronology with the historical record may at times suffer from a similar process of circular argument, as in periods when a historical chronology is available this tends to be highly influential in constructing numismatic chronology, particularly in dating the transition between kings. Numismatic chronology can be particularly effective in assessing economic and political ties during periods of frequent turnover of rulers, as in the 820s where there are five Mercian rulers, Coenwulf, Ceolwulf, Beornwulf, Ludeca and Wiglaf, all of whom minted coinage, recorded in the *Anglo-Saxon Chronicle* in the space of ten years (Bately 1986; Capper 2003; Capper 2008). In contrast, this may be problematic where historical sources fail to acknowledge contested control for example during inter-regna. Pinning down chronological developments in coinage within the longer reigns, such as that of Offa, or in areas which appear to have been incompletely monetised such as central Mercia can be extremely difficult (Chick 2005, 111-21). However, through analysis changes in the design and metal content of numismatic issues, evidence of die linking or from hoards numismatists have presented alternative chronologies for

---

[7] The First Viking Age is usually taken as the phase following the first written account of Viking activity until the Danish settlement of Normandy by Rollo – 793-911 AD. The archaeological phasing usually consists of Early (450-650), Middle (650-850) and Late Saxon (850-1066). My project on the Kingdom of East Anglia considered the period c.700 to c.950 to encompass internal horizons: c.700 x c.730 there is an important horizon in the material culture of the various kingdoms with the end of furnished inhumation burial, but also in East Anglia in the rise of Ipswich wares being mass produced and distributed; to finish at c.950 allowed the full resolution of the East Anglian Kingdom into a Danish entity and then the consolidation of the conquest of that entity by the West Saxons under Edward the Elder and Aethelstan, a period which aimed to extend understandings of West Saxon takeover by encompassing the first minting of coinage under West Saxon royal control in the 930s.

some kingdoms poorly attested in the written sources at times during the Anglo-Saxon period, which demonstrate that alternative chronologies need to be acknowledged and reconciled. H. E. Pagan's synthesis of East Anglian coinage provided a vital re-evaluation of the kingship between 749 and 869, as he was able to demonstrate the re-emergence of a valid East Anglian kingship in ninth century, visible through coinage, but not mentioned in written sources, in the years after the collapse of Mercian hegemony (Pagan 1982).[8] Pagan established a broad chronology for these historically-unattested kings of East Anglia based on cross referencing the contents of coin hoards (Pagan 1982, 42-6).[9] A similar but less accepted chronology was established by Pagan for Northumbria in the ninth century, one which conflicted with the only available historical resources, two post-Conquest historical works believed to have some pre-Conquest material, themselves not independent of each other: Symeon of Durham's *On the Origins and Progress of This the Church of Durham* and the more notorious Roger of Wendover's *Flowers of History* (Pagan 1969; Rollason 2003, 196 n. 29). This numismatic chronology has been challenged more effectively in recent years by Elizabeth J. Pirie, but remains a difficulty in Northumbrian political chronology (Grierson and Blackburn 1986, 302; Lyon 1987; Pirie 1987, 109; 1996a; 1996b; Rollason 1998, 54-62). More recently, coin evidence for continuity of East Anglian kingship following the Viking invasion of 869, which has become established in numismatic circles, contradicted the evidence of the historical sources; namely the *Anglo-Saxon Chronicle* and *Life of Saint Edmund*, that the last native king of the East Angles was Edmund, who was famously killed in winter 869 (Blackburn 2001; Capper 2003; 2008). I was able to use this evidence to reconstruct a very different narrative for the end of the takeover of the East Anglian kingdom by the Danes (Capper 2003, 34).[10] Thus it seems that numismatic evidence has been used to date archaeological excavations, but numismatic chronologies have been unable to impact on debate in other disciplines unless historical sources are unreliable or non-existent.

The potential of the chronologies in different disciplines to profoundly affect one another in the medieval period was recognised in the dedication of the first volume of the York Excavation to historical written sources, analysing them for history, chronology, topography and archaeology: 'at best they can provide information that non-written sources cannot, and at worst they can be a misleading and distorting influence in the analysis' (Rollason 1998, 1). It seems likely that framing interdisciplinary investigation in thematic discussions involving relative rather than specific chronology may enable some of the problems of integrating a specific chronology to be avoided. However, in analysing historical and archaeological research and in questioning the causal relationship between historical and archaeological events, horizons and processes, an integrated approach to chronology may have to be considered. The broader question of how events relate to processes of change in the past has a unique significance in the material comparison used in interdisciplinary methodologies.

The impact of professionalism in formulating and recording the material record

The extent to which unpublished or partly published material influences disciplinary practices has become increasingly important. Colin Renfrew (1980, 295) once said that excavation was unwarranted unless comprehensive publication was undertaken, but as outlined above, due to the constraints of funding in some areas and pressures of statutory requirements such as PPG16 and the Treasure Act in others, some exponents within medieval studies now operate very significantly in an unpublished disciplinary context. In the case of Anglo-Saxon England, as well as the usual conference literature, the influence of grey literature and the volumes of archaeological material already influencing disciplinary practice whilst still in press as 'forthcoming' due to lack of funds include the major chronological repositioning of Middle Saxon East Anglia by Paul Blinkhorn's Ipswich ware project. In numismatics, history and archaeology internet database projects with major implications for Early Medieval Britain are increasingly more fundable than paper based projects (see www.[6], www.[7], www.[8], www.[9]). These sorts of material will be contributed to differently according to regional context or organisation. In short it is as important now as ever before for interdisciplinary researchers to be aware of and to be embedded to some extent in contemporary advances which are occurring within their own disciplinary frameworks, as well as to be actively investigating trends in other disciplines. Further to this point, a recognition of

---

[8] From the end of the hegemony of Ludeca of Mercia over East Anglia, Pagan was able to identify three East Anglian kings. These were provided with admittedly inexact chronological ranges through the number of coin types and by the cross-referencing of moneyers and hoard contents with historically datable coinages of other Anglo-Saxon kings. Of three known kings to AD 869, two were historically unattested: Aethelstan from c.827 then Aethelweard, then Eadmund from c.855 who was killed by Vikings in winter 869 (870). *The Chronicle of John of Worcester* and the *Annals of St Neots* date the reign of Eadmund from 855, but it is notable that Abbo of Fleury's original earlier tenth-century *passio* did not date the succession of Eadmund (Darlington and McGurk 1995, 275 n.5). Marion Archibald (1982) has since argued that the evidence of a ship type of Aethelstan and other more varied coin types may push the date for his contesting Mercian rule back further.

[9] It was important for this work that three moneyers who had previously minted for Mercian kings – Eadgar, Aethelnoth and Monn – also minted coins of Aethelstan for East Anglia, which demonstrates that these were not later coins of the Danish East Anglian king Guthrum, who was also named Aethelstan. The use of the title 'REX ANG' for *Rex Anglorum* demonstrates Aethelstan's claim to full kingship of the East Angles. The principle hoards used, given with Pagan's dating, are the Delgany Hoard, c.828, London Middle Temple hoard, c.840, Dorking hoard c.862, Gravesend hoard, c.871 and Croyden hoard c.874.

[10] In my MA thesis I argued that the continued evidence of East Anglian rulership under Danish influence was crucial in interpreting the gap between Edmund's death described in the *Chronicle* in 869 and in the

Passio Sancti Eadmundi and Guthrum's departure into East Anglia after Edington in 878.

the increasing potential of collaborative research in the humanities and the role of the research environment to postgraduate study was recognised by the Arts and Humanities Research Council in their first round of Collaborative Doctoral Awards in 2005 and recently in the funding available for collaborative research training (www.[10]). There may be a need to consider more fully the applicability of collaborative PhD projects to current medieval research questions and the practical potential and implications of funding joint supervision.

Medieval theory?

The interaction between texts and artefacts, for example as discussed by John Moreland (2001), is one aspect of practice that is fundamental to the pursuit of the inter-relation between archaeology and history and fundamental to the study of the medieval period. Often one piece of material culture can be investigated from multiple disciplinary methods, for example in the case of a coin through a study of findspot, fabric, inscription, textual relationships and so forth. An awareness of the multidisciplinary interest in medieval studies, the sparseness of evidence and the cross fertilization of ideas, has at times called into question the status of those engaged in medieval studies within the disciplines of Archaeology and History; the opposition between theory and practice may have been particularly felt in the case of historical archaeologists (Johnson 1999, 31-4). Reflective consideration suggests that the openness of medieval studies to interdisciplinary perspectives limits the possibility of maintaining the separateness of disciplinary records in any case; by appreciating the subconscious effect of working in an environment where interdisciplinary awareness is a truism, the most constructive response would be to accept and manage the relationship rather than call into question the fidelity of practitioners to their own disciplines. Part of this may be negotiated by a more active consideration and awareness of the pull of disciplinary and period specific preferences in the use of theory.

Historical and archaeological data and arguments and literary and anthropological models can lose much of their value or cohesiveness when taken out of their original context. As concepts travel between disciplines, the language in which the theories of the different disciplines are expressed, the same words, can have very different connotations (Bal 2002, 24). Edmund Leach understood long ago the issues raised by different frameworks of reference, he pointed out that 'before we can agree upon a problem we must first establish a common language of discourse and that may be very difficult' (Leach 1979, 119). It may be that some categories of medieval life might require a specifically medieval consideration, something that I think can provoke further discussion. For example we might consider the institutions of early medieval kingship, the spatial restrictions of serfdom, or the cultural position of paganism or slavery as particularly medieval perspectives, very unlike apparently similar themes in other periods, genuinely requiring consideration in their own context, and for example the concept of 'feudalism' as requiring particular 'medieval' insight. In contrast, medieval concepts of identity, the gendered position of men and women and the body have already been closely linked to theory from other disciplines and periods (Brubaker and Smith 2004; Bynum 1995; Foot 1996; Hadley 1999; Nelson 1997). Some attempts at theorising the Middle Ages across those disciplines involved have proved interesting, but potentially difficult in terms of their theoretical applicability, as with the application of postcolonial theories (Cohen 2000; 2003; Meehan and Townsend 2001). It is still a matter of debate whether the alterity of the Middle Ages should prevent the application of theoretical concepts related to non-contemporary structures across periods as anachronistic, for example the teleological complications of using the term 'state' to describe medieval polities (Davis 1998; Reynolds 1997). Whilst anachronism can stimulate new ways of thinking, at times theoretical borrowing may obscure more than it reveals. Is it reasonable to distort the record of the medieval past, and if so how far, for the sake of confronting a current theoretical framework such as postcolonialism? I would argue that we need to consider very seriously Gabrielle Spiegel's (2000) call for fidelity to medieval modes of thought. Spiegel writes in the context of a review of Kathleen Biddick's work in which, amongst other applications, Biddick applied Holocaust trauma theory to the subdiscipline of medieval history itself. In countering this, Spiegel (ibid., 247) highlights the need for 'fidelity to medieval categories of thought and experience' and for the 'historical specificity and density' (ibid., 250) of a theoretical model to be considered before it is applied. Likewise, in considering medieval theories grounded in medieval examples we might avoid not only anachronistic interpretations, but also oversimplifying the medieval past if, as Edward Said asserted, anthropology can also act as a flawed tool which re-constructs orientalism through the oversimplification of oriental cultures (Said 1978 [reprinted 1991], 259). Furthermore, if as Gabrielle Spiegel (2000, 246) points out 'it seems reasonable to request that the relevance of theory for medieval history be demonstrated before it is implemented', then does it not also follow that to integrate the evidence produced or analysed under different disciplines, the theory or methodology which has assessed other evidence types should be known and considered before the evidence is included? Likewise, having developed a more complete understanding of the potential to theorise the interaction of archaeological and historical approaches and narratives for medieval society, might this not lead to more cohesive theoretical paradigms which can influence the application of balanced theoretical approaches elsewhere, in other disciplines or especially in other historical periods?

Preliminary conclusions

Interdisciplinary awareness in the study of the medieval past is reflected both in current theory and practice. The question of how disciplines studying the past relate to each other, and the methodology governing how the bodies of evidence they produce are made to interact, should probably be considered more actively. This is particularly the case given the current trend for rejection of monocausal explanations for past events and processes in favour of more complex interactions between multiple causal factors (Jordanova 2000, 108-9). Certainly, the appropriateness of interdisciplinarity must be considered as fundamental in the early formulation of a research project and establishment of research questions. I would also argue that interdisciplinarity can add important additional perspectives, but that this approach should be used selectively rather than reified. Not all research questions or topics will add significantly more to current knowledge through the use of interdisciplinary approaches and studies may be compromised in other ways. The time-limited nature of most current research project funding may make it particularly imperative on a practical level that an initial study into the feasibility of the question, project resource base and chronological and spatial parameters is undertaken, followed up by effective routine monitoring. In terms of results, the value may be in perpetuating rather than reconciling different interpretations. As in Comparative History, it may be that failure to find commonalities between the paradigms produced by different disciplines may be as important to future research as resolving the conflicts between paradigms. In particular it is vital that as medievalists we consider our use of interdisciplinary materials in such a way as to contribute actively to the dialogue within disciplines as well as amongst ourselves. What I would like to ask that we consider further as researchers is what effect the long term profile of interdisciplinarity in the medieval period will have in engaging positively to elaborate on the relationship between Archaeology and History.

Acknowledgements

Many thanks to Zoë Devlin and Caroline Holas-Clark for inviting me to speak at the 'Approaching Interdisciplinarity' conference, and to all those who attended for their helpful comments. I would like to express my gratitude to my supervisor Professor Sarah Foot and Simona Latimer for their input on earlier drafts of this paper. All mistakes remain the work of the author.

Bibliography

Archibald, M.M. 1982. 'A ship type of Athelstan I of East Anglia', *British Numismatic Journal*, 52: 34-40

Archibald, M.M. 1988. 'English medieval coins as dating evidence', in J. Casey and R. Reece (eds.), *Coins and the Archaeologist*, 2nd ed., Seaby (London): 264-301

Austin, D. 1990. 'The 'proper study' of medieval archaeology', in L. Alcock and D. Austin (eds.), *From the Baltic to the Black Sea: Studies in Medieval Archaeology*, Unwin Hyman (London): 9-42

Bal, M. 2002. *Travelling Concepts in the Humanities: A Rough Guide,* University of Toronto Press (Toronto)

Bately, J. (ed.) 1986. *The Anglo-Saxon Chronicle. A Collaborative Edition, vol. 3 MS. 'A'* (Cambridge)

Binford, L. 1962. 'Archaeology and anthropology', *American Antiquity*, 28: 217-225

Blackburn, M. A. S. 2001. 'Expansion and control. Aspects of Anglo-Scandinavian minting south of the Humber', in *Vikings and the Danelaw: Select Papers from the Proceedings of the Thirteenth Viking Congress, Nottingham and York, 21-30 August 1997*, Oxbow (Oxford): 125-142

Blinkhorn, P. W. forthcoming, *Ipswich Ware*, Medieval Pottery Research Group Occasional Paper

Bloch, M. 1954. *The Historian's Craft*, transl. P. Putnam, Manchester University Press (Manchester)

Bloch, M. 1961. *Feudal Society*, transl. L.A. Manyon, Routledge & Kegan Paul (London)

Brubaker, L. and Smith, J.M.H. (eds.) 2004. *Gender in the Early Medieval World: East and West, 300-900*, Cambridge University Press (Cambridge)

Burke, P. 1990. *The French Historical Revolution, the Annales School, 1929-89*, Polity (Cambridge)

Bynum, C. 1995 'Why all the fuss about the Body? A medievalist's perspective', *Critical Inquiry*, 22 (1): 1-33

Capper, M.D.T. 2003. *Insights from obscurity. The Anglo-Saxon Kingdom of East Anglia (c. 700-950)*, unpublished MA Dissertation, University of Sheffield

Capper, M.D.T. 2005. 'Insights from obscurity: interdisciplinary analysis as a key to the Anglo-Saxon Kingdom of East Anglia', unpublished paper given at The International Medieval Congress, University of Leeds

Capper, M.D.T. 2008. *Contested loyalties, regional and national identities in the midland kingdoms of Anglo-Saxon England, c.700-c.900*, unpublished Ph.D. dissertation, University of Sheffield

Carr, H.E. 1961. *What is History*, Macmillan (London)

Carver, M. 2007. 'Editorial', *Antiquity*, 81 (2): 261-266

Champion, T. 1990. 'Medieval archaeology and the tyranny of the historical record', in L. Alcock and D. Austin (eds.), *From the Baltic to the Black Sea: Studies in Medieval Archaeology*, Unwin Hyman (London): 79-95

Chick, D. 2005. 'The coinage of Offa in the light of recent discoveries', in D. Hill and M. Worthington (eds.), *Aethelbald and Offa: Two Eighth-Century Kings of Mercia*, B.A.R., British Series, 383 (Oxford): 111-121

Clanchy, M. 1970. 'Remembering the past and the good old law', *History*, 55: 165-176

Clanchy, M. 1979. *From Memory to Written Record; England 1066-1307*, Blackwell (London)

Cohen, J.J. (ed.) 2000. *The Post Colonial Middle Ages*, Palgrave (New York)

Cohen, J.J. (ed.) 2003. *Medieval Identity Machines*, University of Minnesota Press (Minneapolis)

Coonin, B. 2003. 'Grey literature: an annotated bibliography', prepared by the STS Subject & Bibliographic Access Committee Association of College and Research Libraries [online], http://personal.ecu.edu/cooninb/Greyliterature.htm (accessed 1 January 2007)

Curta, F. 2007. 'Some remarks on ethnicity in medieval archaeology', *Early Medieval Europe*, 15 (2): 159-185

Darlington R.R. and McGurk, P. (eds.) 1995. Chronicon Johannis Wigorniensis: *The Chronicle of John of Worcester, Vol. 2: The Annals from 450 to 1066*, Oxford Medieval Texts (Oxford)

Darvill, T. and Russell, B. (eds.) 2002. *Archaeology after PPG16: archaeological investigations in England 1990-1999*, Bournemouth University in association with English Heritage (Bournemouth and London) [online], http://csweb.bournemouth.ac.uk/aip/ppg16/ppg16.htm (accessed 1 March, 2007)

Davis, K. 1998. 'National writing in the ninth century: a reminder for postcolonial thinking about the nation', *Journal of Medieval and Early Modern Studies*, 28: 611-37

Dumville, D.N. 1987. 'Textual archaeology and Northumbrian history subsequent to Bede', in D.M. Metcalf (ed.), *Coinage in Ninth-Century Northumbria. The Tenth Oxford Symposium on Monetary History*, B.A.R., British Series, 180 (Oxford): 43-55

Endersby, J.W. 1996. 'Collaborative research in the social sciences: multiple authorship and publication credit', *Social Science Quarterly*, 77 (2): 375-392

Evans Pritchard, E.E. 1937. *Witchcraft, Oracles and Magic among the Azande*, Clarendon Press (Oxford)

Falkingham, G. 2005. 'A whiter shade of grey: a new approach to archaeological grey literature using the XML version of the TEI Guidelines', *Internet Archaeology*, 17 [online], http://intarch.ac.uk/journal/issue17/5/gf1-1to1-3.html (accessed 1 May 2007)

Foot, S. 1996. 'The making of *Angelcynn*: English identity before the Norman Conquest', *Transactions of the Royal Historical Society*, sixth series, 6: 25-49

Foot, S. 2005. 'On being early', inaugural lecture given at the University of Sheffield [online], http://www.shef.ac.uk/hri/news/inagural.html (accessed 1 January, 2007)

Fryde E.B. (ed.) 1986. *Handbook of British Chronology*, 3rd edition, Royal Historical Society (London)

Geary, P. 1986. 'Sacred commodities: the circulation of medieval relics', in A. Appadurai (ed.), *The Social Life of Things; Commodities in Cultural Perspective*, Cambridge University Press (Cambridge): 169-191

Germano, W.P. 1999. 'Why interdisciplinarity isn't enough', in M. Bal (ed.), *The Practice of Cultural Analysis. Exposing Interdisciplinary Interpretation*, Stanford University Press (Stanford, Ca.): 327-334

Goffart, W.A. 1988. *The Narrators of Barbarian History (AD 550-800: Jordanes, Gregory of Tours, Bede, and Paul the Deacon)*, Princeton University Press (Princeton)

Goodman, J. 1997. 'History and anthropology', in M. Bentley (ed.), *Companion to Historiography*, Routledge (London & New York): 783-804

Grierson, P. and Blackburn, M.A.S. 1986. *Medieval European Coinage, 1: The Early Middle Ages (5th-10th centuries)*, Cambridge University Press (Cambridge)

Hadley, D.M. 1999. *Masculinity in Medieval Europe*, Longman (London & New York)

Hadley, D.M. and Richards, J.D. 2000. 'Introduction: interdisciplinary approaches to the Scandinavian settlement', in D.M. Hadley and J.D. Richards (eds.), *Cultures in Contact; Scandinavian Settlement in England in the Ninth and Tenth Centuries*, Studies in the Early Middle Ages 2, Brepols (Turnhout): 3-15

Halsall, G. 1997. 'Archaeology and historiography', in M. Bentley (ed.), *Companion to Historiography*, Routledge (London & New York): 805-827

Heffner, A.G. 1979. 'Authorship recognition of subordinates in collaborative research', *Social Studies in Science*, 9 (3): 377-384

Higham N.J. 1999, 'East Anglia', in M. Lapidge (ed.), *The Blackwell Encyclopaedia of Anglo-Saxon England*, Blackwell (Oxford): 155

Hills, C. 2007. 'History and archaeology: the state of play in early medieval Europe', *Antiquity*, 81 (1): 191-200

Hines, J., Høilund Nielsen, K. and Siegmund, F. (eds.) 1999. *The Pace of Change. Studies in Early Medieval Chronology*, Oxbow (Oxford)

Hitchener, B. 1994. 'The merits and challenges of an *Annaliste* approach to archaeology', *Journal of Roman Archaeology*, 7: 408-17

Hobsbawm, E.J. 1979. 'An historian's comments', in *Space, Hierarchy and Society; Interdisciplinary Studies in Social Area Analysis*, B.A.R., International Series, 59 (Oxford): 247-252

Hodder, I. 1982. *Symbols in Action. Ethnoarchaeological Studies of Material Culture*, Cambridge University Press (Cambridge)

Hodder, I. 1986. *Reading the Past*, Cambridge University Press (Cambridge)

Hodder, I. 1995. 'Material culture in time', in I. Hodder, M. Shanks, A. Alexandri, V. Buchli, J. Carman, J. Last and G. Lucas (eds.), *Interpreting Archaeology. Finding Meanings in the Past*, Routledge (London): 164-168

Hodges, R. 2006. *Goodbye to the Vikings. Re-reading Early Medieval Archaeology*, Duckworth (London)

Johnson, M.H. 1999. 'Rethinking historical archaeology', in P.P.A. Funari, M. Hall and S. Jones (eds.), *Historical Archaeology. Back From the Edge*, Routledge (London & New York): 23-36

Jordanova, L. 1992. 'Resisting reflexivity', *The History of the Human Sciences*, 5: 59-67

Jordanova, L. 2000. *History in Practice*, Arnold (London)

Karp I. and Lavine, S.D. (eds.) 1991. *Exhibiting Cultures: the Poetics and Politics of Museum Display*, Smithsonian Press (Washington, D.C.)

Kopytoff, I. 1986. 'The cultural biography of things: commoditization as process', in A. Appadurai (ed.), *The Social Life of Things. Commodities in Cultural Perspective*, Cambridge University Press (Cambridge): 64-91

Layton, R.H. (ed.) 1989. *Conflict in the Archaeology of Living Traditions*, One World Archaeology, Unwin Hyman (London)

Leach, E. 1979. 'Discussion', in B.C. Burnham, and J. Kingsbury (eds.), *Space, Hierarchy and Society; Interdisciplinary Studies in Social Area Analysis*, B.A.R., International Series, 59 (Oxford): 119-124

Leone, M. 1988. 'The relationship between archaeological data and the documentary record: 18th-century gardens in Annapolis, Maryland', *Historical Archaeology*, 22: 29-35

Loyn, H. 1991. 'The Howard Linecar Lecture 1990. Numismatics and the medieval historian: A comment on recent numismatic contributions to the history of England', *British Numismatic Journal*, 60: 29-36

Lyon, S. 1987. 'Ninth-century chronology', in D.M. Metcalf (ed.), *Coinage in Ninth-Century Northumbria; the Tenth Oxford Symposium on Coinage and Monetary History*, B.A.R., British Series, 180 (Oxford): 27-41

McKitterick, R. 1990. 'Introduction', in R. McKitterick (ed.), *The Uses of Literacy in Early Medieval Europe*, Cambridge University Press (Cambridge): 1-10

Meehan, U. and Townsend, D. 2001. '"Nation" and the gaze of the other in eighth-century Northumbria', *Comparative Literature*, 53 (1): 1-26

Moreland, J. 2001. *Archaeology and Text*, Duckworth (London)

Nelson, J.L. 1997. 'Family, gender and sexuality in the Middle Ages', in M. Bentley (ed.), *Companion to Historiography*, Routledge (London & New York): 153-76

Nelson, J.L. 2002. 'England and the continent in the ninth century: I, Ends and beginnings', *Transactions of the Royal Historical Society*, sixth series, 12: 1-21

Oosthuizen, S. 2005. 'New lights on the origins of open-field farming', *Medieval Archaeology*, 49: 165-93.

Pagan, H.E. 1969. 'Northumbrian numismatic chronology in the ninth century', *British Numismatic Journal*, 38: 1-15

Pagan, H.E. 1982. 'The coinage of the East Anglian kingdom from 825 to 870', *British Numismatic Journal*, 52: 41-83

Pestell, T. 2004. *Landscapes of Monastic Foundation: The Establishment of Religious Houses in East Anglia, c.650-1200*, Boydell & Brewer, Ltd. (Woodbridge)

Pirie, E.J.E. 1987. 'Phases and groups within the Styca coinage of Northumbria', in D.M. Metcalf (ed.), *Coinage in Ninth-Century Northumbria; the Tenth Oxford Symposium on Coinage and Monetary History*, B.A.R., British Series, 180 (Oxford): 103-145

Pirie, E.J.E. 1996a. 'Eardwulf: a significant addition to the coinage of Northumbria, *British Numismatic Journal*, 65: 20-31

Pirie, E.J.E. 1996b. *Coins of the Kingdom of Northumbria c.700-867 in the Yorkshire Collections: the Yorkshire Museum, York, the University of Leeds, the City Museum, Leeds*, Galata Press (Llanfyllin)

Poole, R.L. 1921. *Medieval Reckonings of Time*, Society for Promoting Christian Knowledge (London)

Remensnyder, A.G. 2002. 'Topographies of memory: center and periphery in High Medieval France', in G. Althoff, J. Fried, P. Geary (eds.), *Medieval Concepts of the Past: Ritual, Memory, Historiography*, Cambridge University Press (Cambridge): 193-214

Renfrew, C. 1980. 'The great tradition versus the great divide: archaeology as anthropology?', *American Journal of Archaeology*, 84 (3): 287-298

Reuter, T. 1998. 'Medieval: another tyrannous construct?', *The Medieval History Journal*, 1: 25-45

Reuter, T. 2006. 'Medieval mentalities and modern polities', in J.L. Nelson (ed.), *Medieval Polities and Modern Mentalities*, Cambridge University Press (Cambridge): 3-18

Reynolds, S. 1997. 'The historiography of the medieval state', in M. Bentley (ed.), *Companion to Historiography*, Routledge (London & New York): 117-138

Rollason, D.W. with Gore, D. and Fellows-Jensen, G. 1998. *Sources for York History to AD 1100*, The Archaeology of York, vol. 1, York Archaeological Trust, (York)

Rollason, D.W. 2003. *Northumbria, 500-1100; Creation and Destruction of a Kingdom*, Cambridge University Press (Cambridge)

Said, E. 1978 [1991]. *Orientalism*, Pantheon Books (New York)

Scull, C. and Bayliss, A. 1999. 'Radiocarbon dating and Anglo-Saxon graves', in U. von Freeden, U. Koch and A Wieczorek (eds.), *Völker an Nord- und Ostsee und die Franken: Akten des 48. Sachsensymposiums in Mannheim vom 7. bis 11. September 1997*, Habelt (Bonn): 39-50

Spiegel, G. 1997 *The Past as Text, the Theory and Practice of Medieval Historiography*, Johns Hopkins University Press (Baltimore and London)

Spiegel, G. 2000. 'Epater les Medievistes', *History and Theory*, 39: 243-250

Stenton, F.M. 1971. *Anglo-Saxon England*, 3rd ed., Oxford University Press (Oxford)

Thomas, K. 1963. 'History and anthropology', *Past and Present*, 24: 9-14

Thomas, K. 1970. 'The relevance of social anthropology to the historical study of English witchcraft', in M. Douglas (ed.), *Witchcraft Confessions & Accusations*, Association of Social Anthropologists of the Commonwealth, Monograph 9, Tavistock Publications (London): 47-79

Thomas, K. 1971. *Religion and the Decline of Magic; Studies in Popular Beliefs in Sixteenth- and Seventeenth-Century England*, Weidenfeld & Nicolson (New York)

Tilley, C. 1991. *Material Culture and Text. The Art of Ambiguity*, Routledge (London & New York)

Tilley, C. (ed.) 1993. *Interpretative Archaeology*, Berg (Providence, R.I. & Oxford)

Trigger, B. 2006. *History of Archaeological Thought*, 2nd ed., Cambridge University Press (Cambridge)

Wade, K. 2001. 'Gipeswic: East Anglia's first economic capital, 600-1066', in N. Salmon and R. Malster (eds.), *Ipswich from the First to the Third Millennium* (Ipswich): 1-6

Weintraub, I. 2000. 'The role of grey literature in the Sciences' [online], http://library.brooklyn.cuny.edu/access/greyliter.htm (accessed 1 May 2007)

Wickham, C. 2005. *Framing the Early Middle Ages, Europe and the Mediterranean, 400-800*, Oxford University Press (Oxford)

www.[1] *What is PPG16?* [online], http://www.archaeology.co.uk/further/gateway/ppghome.htm (accessed 1 March 2007)

www.[2] *ppg16: a brave new world or, a busted knacker?* [online discussion forum], http://www.bajr.org/bajrforum/topic.asp?ARCHIVE=true&TOPIC_ID=154 (accessed 1 September, 2006)

www.[3] Portable Antiquities Scheme, Summary of the Treasure Act [online], http://www.finds.org.uk/treasure/treasure_summary.php (accessed 1 April 2006)

www.[4] The Open University [online], http://library.open.ac.uk/resources/reports.html (accessed 1 May 2007)

www.[5] 'From the ground up. The publication of archaeological reports, a user needs survey', Council for British Archaeology [online], http://www.britarch.ac.uk/pubs/puns/punsrep4.html (accessed 1 April 2007)

www.[6] Corpus of Early Medieval Coin Finds [online], Fitzwilliam Museum, Cambridge, http://www.fitzmuseum.cam.ac.uk/coins/emc

www.[7] 'The Portable Antiquities Scheme' [online], http://www.finds.org.uk/background/aboutus.php

www.[8] 'Prosopography of Anglo Saxon England' [online], http://www.pase.ac.uk/

www.[9] 'The Lands of the Normans in England (1204-44)' [online], http://www.shef.ac.uk/history/research/projects/normans.html

www.[10] Arts and Humanities Research Council, http://www.ahrb.ac.uk/university_staff/postgraduate.asp#1 (accessed 1 May 2007)

Zieman Davis, N. 1981. 'Anthropology and history in the 1980s; the possibilities of the past', *Journal of Interdisciplinary History*, 12 (2): 267-275

Zuckerman, H.A. 1968. 'Patterns of name ordering among authors of scientific papers: a study of social symbolism and its ambiguity', *American Journal of Sociology*, 74: 276-91

Archaeology, history and economics: exploring everyday life in Anglian Deira

Caroline Holas-Clark

Rather than presenting examples from my research, my aim in this paper is to reflect on the experiences I have had using evidence from both textual sources and material culture in the context of my doctoral research. I will start by introducing the historical and archaeological sources that form the basis of my project. The next section of the paper will discuss the reasons for my choice of Deira, and the Anglian period, between 700 and 867 as my research focus. This provides a context for the evaluation of the interdisciplinary approach that I have used. As I am currently preparing the final draft of my thesis, the challenges that my research has encountered are particularly obvious to me; they will, I hope, prove interesting to others as well. However, the rewards of interdisciplinarity are considerable, and I will conclude by outlining the ultimate potential of an interdisciplinary methodology for economic history.

Section I: Introduction to sources

The historical sources for the Anglo-Saxon kingdom of Northumbria come in two phases, characterized by extremities of scale. For the period up until 731, there is the detailed testimony of perhaps the greatest historical source of the early middle ages, the *Historia Ecclesiastica Gentis Anglorum* written by the Venerable Bede in Bernicia (Colgrave and Mynors 1969), the northern of the two polities which were united to form the kingdom of Northumbria. Numerous other textual sources illuminate the Northumbrian history of the seventh, and particularly the eighth, centuries, including a significant body of hagiography and various other ecclesiastical documentation, as discussed in the wide-ranging conference proceedings on *Northumbria's Golden Age* (Hawkes and Mills 1999). The works of Alcuin, the second of Anglo-Saxon Northumbria's most renowned scholarly sons, recently examined in detail by Donald Bullough (2004), seal this treasure trove of textual riches. Alcuin produced a poetic celebration of the history of York and a weighty body of correspondence (Dümmler 1895), mostly written in the second stage of his career, when he lived in Francia under the patronage of the emperor Charlemagne.

For the years from Alcuin's death at the start of the ninth century to the end of the Viking kingdom of Jorvík, however, there is a scholarly silence north of the Humber. Basic facts emerge from a patchwork of sources, including Anglo-Saxon material from southern England and texts written after the Norman conquest, particularly in the historically-focused environment of eleventh-century Durham (for discussion see Rollason 1998). Such texts allow the construction of a basic historical framework, although there is no bridging many gaps and little obvious way around numerous inconsistencies, an inevitable consequence of the diverse, and occasionally downright unreliable, nature of the surviving record.

The extremities of textual survival are mirrored in the material sources for the region. The most dramatic, perhaps, is the numismatic record. Northumbria has a respectable corpus of coins from the eighth century, which duly attest the kings and archbishops who feature in the historical sources. However, a momentous decision was taken by Northumbrian coin-issuing authorities in the early ninth century, which dramatically increased the volume of the region's coinage preserved until modern times. This decision was the apparently deliberate abandonment of silver as a coinage medium, and its replacement with a high-zinc copper alloy, which has been the focus of considerable academic interest (see especially articles in Metcalf 1987). Although these brass coins, generally known as *styca*s, would have been attractive as well as practical, it is inherently likely that they were not worth nearly as much as a silver coin. Their lower denominational value is likely to have been a major part of their phenomenal success, and activity by metal-detecting enthusiasts has produced hundreds of single finds of these coins, from East Anglia and Lincolnshire as well as sites within Yorkshire, where they are likely to have been produced. A cluster of hoards form a seal on this extraordinary numismatic episode similar to that of the works of Alcuin for the textual sources. The exact date of this seal is a matter of debate. It would be obvious, and neat, to date the end of the *styca* coinage to the conventional Viking conquest of York in 867 – but the very tidiness of such an attribution is perhaps a warning that it might be unreliable. The coins themselves suggest a more concrete problem: coins issued by kings who are thought to have reigned in the later 850s and 860s survive in significantly fewer numbers than issues of the 840s. In any case, the collapse of the coinage took no more than three decades: in the 840s, the type was in its prime, with hundreds, if not thousands, of coins issued each year. By the 870s it is probable that the *styca*s were obsolete, with little economic value beyond their tiny volume of copper-alloy bullion.

A significant amount of other information from Anglo-Saxon Yorkshire can be added to this wealth, then dearth, of Northumbrian textual material, and sudden, though brief, blossoming of a high-volume coinage. The publication of Anglian levels from four major research excavations – at Beverley (Armstrong 1991), Cottam (Richards 1999), several sites in the deserted medieval village of Wharram Percy (Milne and Richards 1992; Croft and Stamper 2000) and the Fishergate site in York (Rogers 1993) – has provided a wealth of archaeological material dating to the seventh and eighth centuries, including evidence of settlement activity and assemblages of artefacts such as pottery, metalwork and animal bones, each of which have been subject to detailed scrutiny by specialists in the appropriate field. The city of York and the North East Riding of Yorkshire have also been covered in volumes of the *Corpus of Anglo-Saxon Stone Sculpture*, making another hugely valuable source easily accessible to non-specialist research (Lang 1991 and 2001).

Section Two: Background to my research and discussion of study region and period

In fact, the biggest problem that has emerged with an interdisciplinary approach to the region is one that will, I am sure, be familiar to many of us – time. No interdisciplinary study can approach source material with the in-depth approach of a specialist. It is therefore tempting to simply accept without question the interpretation of specialist reports, and there is, indeed, much value in simply being aware of the material. However, much more value can be gained from specialist reports by acquiring enough expertise to understand the primary data presented in them directly, so that the interpretation offered can be properly evaluated. This kind of truly interdisciplinary approach is a gamble – it involves the investment of a considerable amount of research time acquiring new skills rather than undertaking primary research. However, in order to truly access research from fields of study outside that in which a researcher has been trained, such investments are necessary. Few interpretations are definitive; evidence from the early medieval world is not often convincingly reduced to textbook answers, so an understanding of the argument on which specialist conclusions are built is essential in order to use those conclusions with sensitivity. In any case, the odds of the interdisciplinary gamble are less than they might appear, as simply bringing evidence together from different areas of study almost always provides novel insights, and they are reduced still further when study topics are chosen to maximise both the quantity and quality of the evidence available to the project.

This brings me, finally, to the project that I have undertaken in my own thesis. My undergraduate and Masters training focused on the historical and literary sources of Anglo-Saxon England. Detailed study of charter material combined with my West Riding background led to a Masters dissertation examining charters and land tenure in northern England (Smith 2001). However, deeper economic questions beckoned – what did people actually do with the land? What did it mean to live in Anglo-Saxon Northumbria for those who were not involved in the dynastic struggles that seem to have occupied the aristocracy, or the full-time moralising that seems to have occupied the clergy? What did the Northumbrian representatives of the least glamorous of King Alfred's triumvirate of medieval society, 'those that worked', actually do?

The textual wealth of eighth-century Northumbria and the numismatic wealth of the ninth convinced me that much could be gained from a regional study. Several reasons led to my focus on Deira, the southern of Northumbria's two regions. The most basic was the need to reduce the scope to something more manageable in a course of doctoral study than the vast geographical spread of Anglo-Saxon Northumbria. The amount of specialist research already undertaken meant that Deira showed great potential, as the interdisciplinary approach I have used is completely dependent on the pre-existence of specialist analysis. The writings of Bede and the eighth-century hagiographers have been a major focus of historical research for many years, and although the Deiran focus distanced the project from important Bedan and hagiographical texts, many of their insights do appear more generally Northumbrian than immediately local. Archaeological research on individual sites, however, is specific to the locality, and the volume and range of published excavations from sites within Deira was striking. The coinage of Anglo-Saxon Northumbria has also been subject to detailed specialist study, and the numismatic history of the region has been reconstructed in some detail. All of this specialist publication provided a means of accessing the rich resources available without specialist training in individual disciplines, making Deira an ideal case-study to trial an interdisciplinary approach.

Having established a regional focus, it was necessary to consider the issue of the proposed study period. The start date was a largely practical one – the turn of the eighth century marked the appearance of the rich Northumbrian textual corpus discussed above, while encompassing a good range of archaeological sites. The year 700 also seemed a convenient date historically, coming after what Bede would suggest to have been several decades of political and religious stability. This suggested a helpful set of basic assumptions: the population was likely to have been basically Christian, for example, and the unity of Deira with Bernicia was already of some antiquity, and as secure as it was perhaps ever to become.

The establishment of the end-date of the project, however, was less straightforward. The complexities of English involvement in Northumbria in the later tenth and eleventh centuries appeared immediately too remote from the early material to form part of the same project. However, the original end-date was set around 920, to include an assessment of the economic impact of Scandinavian conquest. This was one of the interdisciplinary gambles that essentially failed, although with some irony as the failure was due to it being too good a question, with too much evidence available to answer it. I had already invested considerable research time before I reluctantly came to the conclusion that it was not going to be feasible to consider the economy of the later ninth and early tenth centuries in any depth within my doctoral research. The scope of my project therefore eventually became 'The Economic History of Anglian Deira, AD 700-867' (Smith 2006).

Section 3: Problems

This brings me to a consideration of the problems that I have encountered while pursuing an interdisciplinary approach. The ultimate reduction in the scope of the project was a direct result of my inexperience with many of the sources I was using: had I had any concept of the sheer quantity of information available, for example, I could have seen much earlier that it was not going to be possible to undertake a serious study of the Anglo-Scandinavian period, and saved myself from considerable unusable research. I would also, no doubt, have made a better job of prioritising. Some priorities were obvious: the *styca* coinage was an obvious focus for the research, and study of the eighth-century historical sources another. However, it has often been hard to anticipate the value of a source, and the research methods that would be needed to approach it, in advance, and the issue of time has never been an easy one. The result has been that sources whose testimony was not immediately obvious ended up with very little time at the end of the project. While this has left me with a long list of follow-up research, the frustration of finding another source with important evidence late in a research project is considerable.

In some ways, an interdisciplinary career is always bound to be a work in progress; there are always more sources which could be considered and, if at all valuable, these sources are bound to modify, if not completely undermine, previous work. Even more alarmingly from the perspective of project management and coherence, more experience with particular kinds of source often leads, in my case at least, to deeper levels of understanding about the insights they can provide. However, this is true of all academic careers: few researchers in any field maintain their initial perspectives for the whole of their professional lives. Changes in theoretical approaches and available data will always be reflected in interdisciplinary work as well as in the specialist research on which it is based.

Another serious practical issue that arose from the interdisciplinary nature of the research was how to present the final report. The most logical way of undertaking the research was to consider each source individually: this allowed for a period of familiarisation with the scholarship and nature of the source, before considering the evidence it provided for economic activity. However, presenting the research in this way would have created a report that would have been hard to understand as it jumped from one source to another, introducing each source, with the economic study almost a digression before moving on to the next source. To avoid this kaleidoscopic effect, I have used a thematic approach to present my thesis, considering economic activity under the headings of production, distribution and consumption. This kind of thematic approach has been used to good effect in previous interdisciplinary studies, although the precise themes chosen are specific to individual projects. Weaving the material together in this way is another practical challenge of interdisciplinary work as it demands a considerable amount of time. In a practical sense, it involves considerably more writing as all the research into individual subjects must be carefully recorded, but the final report must be completely written from scratch, integrating the evidence from all the sources used. The intellectual demands of this kind of integration are not inconsiderable. For my project, it has proved to be an entirely separate stage of research from the final writing of the report, and failure to anticipate this extended my research period considerably.

In addition to the basic research questions, using several different sources presents its own kinds of problem. Dating has been a particular problem for sources from Anglian Deira. The historical sources have been much studied and are relatively closely dated. The coins are also dated within narrow bands as their dating criteria is in the form of the name of the king under whose authority they were issued. The chronology of the kingdom of Northumbria is remarkably unclear, and, happily, beyond the scope of my economic study, but the margins of uncertainty rarely exceed a few years and the relative order of kings is fairly secure. However, some categories of archaeological artefacts are much less closely datable: much metalwork and pottery can only be dated in century ranges, for example, and the exact periods of occupation of settlement sites can rarely be pinned down much more closely than decades. Obviously these sources cannot, in fact, be closely combined in their details, but they do both have information to offer on economic activity in the period 700-867, and working out how to present this information within coherent thematic chapters has presented considerable challenges.

Section 4: Benefits

Considering the problems of interdisciplinary approaches in all their glory might suggest the whole enterprise to be madness. A similar conclusion is inevitable for most ways of approaching the early medieval world. However, the potential of the kind of interdisciplinary study that is the focus of this conference is immense. For economic history, it is perhaps revolutionary. The study of economic activity in the historical period has traditionally been based on documents, particularly administrative records. Detailed statistical analysis of such records has been used to test various mathematical models of historical economies, using approaches adapted from the study of the modern economy. No such documents are available from Anglian Northumbria, and its economy has therefore remained largely mysterious. But, as I hope I have shown, the region does have an extremely valuable, if varied, corpus of sources from the Anglian period, of which the imposing collection of material from single-finds and hoards of the *styca* coinage, at least, provides unequivocally economic data. Animal bone assemblages are among the categories of archaeological material which have proved equally valuable, giving eloquent testimony about patterns of production, distribution and consumption on the settlements from which they were found. Specialist analysis of metalwork, pottery, stone and glass assemblages have all proved valuable for the more general study of economic history.

Conclusion

In fact, this kind of approach is not particularly new: as long ago as 1882, William Cunningham was describing economic history as 'not so much the study of a special class of facts as the study of all the facts of a nation's history from a special point of view'. The challenges of the application of this kind of interdisciplinarity in the 21st century, when 'all the facts' include material as diverse as the anatomy of domestic livestock, the stratigraphy of complex archaeological sites, the chemistry of iron ore extraction and a working knowledge of medieval Latin, are immense. However, the results can be equally rewarding. When fully based in the spectacular advances that have been made in the individual disciplines on which medieval studies is founded, interdisciplinarity can ask new questions, and provide entirely new ways of answering them. Even if the journey is perilous and difficult, it is, indeed, well worth approaching.

Acknowledgments

I would like to gratefully acknowledge the wise and patient support of my supervisors, Prof. Julian Richards and Dr Katy Cubitt who have been an unfailing source of strength throughout my research, and, most especially in this context, my co-organiser of this conference, Zoë Devlin, without whose tireless efforts it is hard to imagine this project ever having reached completion.

Bibliography

Armstrong, P. *et al* (eds.) 1991. *Excavations at Lurk Lane Beverley, 1979-1982*, Sheffield Excavation Reports, 1 (Sheffield)

Bullough, D.A. 2004. *Alcuin: Achievement and Reputation: Being Part of the Ford Lectures Delivered in Oxford in Hilary Term 1980*, Brill (Leiden)

Colgrave B. and Mynors, R.A.B. (eds.) 1969. *Bede's Ecclesiastical History of the English People*, Clarendon Press (Oxford)

Croft, R.A. and Stamper, P.A. (eds.) 2000. *The South Manor Area*, Wharram: A Study of Settlement on the Yorkshire Wolds, 8 (York)

Cunningham, W. 1882. *The Growth of English Industry and Commerce*, Cambridge University Press (Cambridge)

Dümmler, E. (ed.) 1895. *Epistolae Karolini Aevi II*, Monumenta Germaniae Historica Epistolae, 4 (Munich)

Hawkes, J. and Mills, S. (eds.) 1999. *Northumbria's Golden Age*, Sutton Publishing (Stroud)

Lang, J. 1991. *Corpus of Anglo-Saxon Stone Sculpture. Volume 3. York and Eastern Yorkshire*, Oxford University Press for the British Academy (Oxford)

Lang, J. 2001. *Corpus of Anglo-Saxon Stone Sculpture. Volume 6. Northern Yorkshire*, Oxford University Press for the British Academy (Oxford)

Metcalf, D.M. (ed.) 1987. *Coinage in Ninth-Century Northumbria: The Tenth Oxford Symposium on Coinage and Monetary History*, B.A.R., British Series, 180 (Oxford)

Milne, G. and Richards, J.D. (eds.) 1992. *Two Anglo-Saxon Buildings and Associated Finds*, Wharram: A Study of Settlement on the Yorkshire Wolds, Volume VII

Richards, J.D. 1999. 'Cottam: An Anglian and Anglo-Scandinavian settlement on the Yorkshire Wolds', *Archaeological Journal*, 156: 1-110

Rogers, N.S.H. (ed.) 1993. *Anglian and Other Finds from Fishergate*, The Archaeology of York 17: The Small Finds, 9 (London)

Rollason, D.W. (ed.) 1998. *Symeon of Durham: Historian of Durham and the North*, Studies in North-Eastern History, 1 (Stamford)

Smith, C.N.J. 2001. 'The endowments of York and Durham: administrative and political authority in Late Anglo-Saxon Northumbria', unpublished undergraduate dissertation, University of Cambridge

Smith, C.N.J. 2006. *The economic history of Anglian Deira, 700-870*, unpublished Ph.D. dissertation, University of York

The end of Anglo-Saxon furnished burial: an interdisciplinary perspective

Zoë L. Devlin

The disappearance of grave goods from the burials of southern and eastern England during the seventh century has always been seen as a major watershed in social and cultural practices. From the nineteenth century, archaeologists found a ready explanation for this change in practice in the documentary sources and especially in Bede's narrative of the conversion of the Anglo-Saxons to Christianity through the efforts of Augustine and his successors (HE I.23-33; II.2-16; III.1, 7, 21-2, 24, 30; IV.16). It was argued that the change in burial practice was the result of the abandonment of burial rites associated with the old pagan religion and the adoption of rites more closely compatible with Christianity. The notion that furnished burial was somehow incompatible with Christian beliefs has not been widely questioned within early medieval archaeology until comparatively recently. However, there is now a growing recognition that this idea stems more from archaeologists' own assumptions about the nature of early medieval Christianity than from contemporary documentary evidence. Many studies have demonstrated that there is no indication that the Church objected to burial with grave goods or took any interest in burial practices at all before the late tenth century.

This reassessment of the evidence has done much to aid our understanding of Anglo-Saxon burial practices. However, it has also effectively brought an end to the interdisciplinary perspective on the burial practices of the early and middle Anglo-Saxon period. The lack of direct written evidence for the influence of the church on burial practices means that documentary sources are now largely ignored by archaeologists as a source of evidence for people's beliefs and attitudes to the dead before the development of Christian liturgical practices that led to the involvement of the clergy in the funeral during the later Anglo-Saxon period. However, when combined with an anthropological perspective, documentary evidence still has the potential to aid our understanding of Anglo-Saxon burial practices in general and of the end of furnished burial in particular. By examining the meaning of objects in relation to death and burial in this period through all the sources available, we can understand how conversion to a new religion might have led indirectly to such an important change in burial practice.

Changes in Anglo-Saxon burial practices

Despite regional and local variations, burial practices in southern and eastern England during the fifth to seventh centuries share enough similarities to allow us to view them as the product of a particular cultural environment. In the fifth and sixth centuries, often referred to as the Migration Period, people were either cremated and their remains buried in an urn or simply wrapped in cloth, or they were laid out in inhumation graves. The aspect of early Anglo-Saxon burial that has received the most attention from archaeologists is the practice of including objects in the grave with the deceased. In inhumation burials, the body was laid out fully dressed, often with other objects of value placed beside them. Typical assemblages found with women include brooches, bead strings, and items hanging from the waist such as girdle-hangers, keys and latch-lifters (Hines 1992; Owen-Crocker 2004; Stoodley 1999). Men were often inhumed with weapons, including spears, shields and, much more rarely, swords. Knives are the most common item for both men and women and both sexes are also found with other tools, such as spindle whorls with women and fire-lighting equipment with men. Grooming equipment such as tweezers and combs are sometimes present, as are pots and buckets, which were associated with feasting (Härke 1989a; 1989b; 1990; 1992; 1997; Stoodley 1999). The objects interred with the deceased are selected from the repertoire of available items, so a 'full kit' is not always present. Children are found much less frequently with objects than are adults and for them gender-specific equipment is rare (Crawford 1993; 1999; 2000; Lucy 1994; Stoodley 1999). Individuals who were cremated before being buried are found with objects selected from the same range of options. However, the frequency of different types of objects shows significant differences from those found in inhumation burials. Jewellery occurs only infrequently and all weapons are extremely rare. In contrast, grooming equipment, such as tweezers and combs, is found much more frequently in cremation burials than in inhumations and has been argued to be associated with the transformation of the body inherent in the cremation process (Williams 2003; 2007). Grave goods have been shown to be closely related to the identity of the deceased individual, with studies variously showing links to ethnicity, gender, age and social status (for examples of different approaches to this issue see Arnold 1980; Crawford 2000; Hadley and Moore 1998; Härke 1990; Hines 1994; James 1989; Leeds 1913; Lucy 1997; Stoodley 1999).

During the late sixth and early seventh centuries, however, Anglo-Saxon burial practices underwent a series of major changes. During this period, cremation burial disappeared from early medieval cemeteries and we can assume that the practice of cremation itself also ended (Hoggett 2007). Many cemeteries of the Migration Period were abandoned and new ones founded nearby, although this was far from universal and several continued in use into the mid-seventh century or later (Boddington 1990; Faull 1976; Geake 1992; Hyslop 1963; Meaney and Hawkes 1970). At the same time, there were significant changes in the types of grave goods interred with the dead. Jewellery becomes more simple, with bead strings disappearing and the large 'showy' pairs of brooches found in the Migration Period being replaced by single disc brooches with Roman- or Byzantine-influenced designs (Geake 1997; Hoggett 2007). Weapon burial declines steadily, with the rite being considered appropriate for fewer and fewer men in society (Härke 1992). Overall, the practice of burial with objects is also in decline during this period, which is generally referred to as the Conversion Period, or the 'Final Phase' of pagan burial. During the seventh and early eighth century, furnished burial for the majority of the population comes to an end and subsequently only a small minority of graves are found with any objects in them, specifically those of churchmen who were sometimes buried with objects associated with their office, and a small number of burials that have been debatably associated with the Viking invasions (for doubts see Hadley 2001; Halsall 2000).

Conversion to Christianity

Bede's *Historia Ecclesiastica* describes the process by which the different kingdoms of early Anglo-Saxon England accepted Christianity. According to his account, this process began in 597 when Augustine arrived in Kent with forty missionaries sent by Pope Gregory the Great and converted King Æthelbert. According to Bede, the last kingdom to come under Christian rulership, and therefore to be Christian in Bede's eyes, is the Isle of Wight in 686. It has long been recognised that the conversion of the ruler should not be equated with the Christianisation of the population as a whole. However, the correlation of the dating of the conversion in Bede with that of the changes in burial practices has traditionally led to the two being associated with each other. It has been argued that the changes in burial practices of the late sixth and early seventh centuries were the result of the conversion, with the old pagan practices of cremation and furnished burial being gradually abandoned, along with pagan burial grounds, and the foundation of new burial grounds for Christian burial. The fact that the 'old ways' persisted, albeit in a slightly different form, for up to a century or more was taken as indicating the length of time required by the church to stamp them out (Leeds 1913; Lethbridge 1931; 1936; Evison 1956; Hyslop 1963; Meaney and Hawkes 1970; see also Boddington 1990).

More recently, these arguments have been re-examined and to a certain extent overturned. An ever-growing data set of Anglo-Saxon cemeteries has indicated that earlier arguments for the abandonment of Migration Period cemeteries and the foundation of new ones during the late sixth and early seventh centuries applies only to some cemeteries such as those at Winnall, Hampshire; Sancton, East Yorkshire; and Chamberlains Barn, Bedfordshire (Faull 1976; Hyslop 1963, Meaney and Hawkes 1970). At many others, such as Edix Hill, Cambridgeshire; Apple Down, Sussex; and Bradstow School, Broadstairs, Kent, burial continued at 'pagan' cemeteries into the 'Christian' period (Down and Welch 1990; Hogarth 1973; Malim and Hines 1998). While there were undoubtedly significant developments in funerary practices at this time that led to some communities founding new cemeteries, we cannot ascribe the reasons for this to anything as large-scale as the conversion. At the very least, if such changes were due to the influence of the new religion they resulted from different teachings in different areas of the country. However, we should not imagine that the movement to new burial grounds was the result of any concerted attempt by the Church to separate the people from the burial grounds of their pre-Christian ancestors.

Similarly, the assumption that burial with grave goods was incompatible with Christianity has been questioned and the evidence reassessed. It has been pointed out that there is no evidence in the documentary sources to indicate that the Church was concerned about burial with grave goods or that it sought to ban furnished burial (Young 1975, 1977; see also Effros 2002, ch. 3; Hadley 2001; James 1989; Morris 1983). Indeed, the Church seems to have shown little interest in burial practices at all until the end of the Anglo-Saxon period (Bullough 1981; Effros 1997; Gittos 2002; Paxton 1990; Zadora Rio 2003). From the Continent there is ample evidence that burial with grave goods was not incompatible with Christianity (cf., Halsall forthcoming 2009). Indeed, it has been noted that the Franks only began furnished burial at the time of their conversion (Halsall forthcoming 2009, 282; James 1988; 1989). In Merovingian Gaul, burial in churches began earlier than in Anglo-Saxon England, with some examples from the second quarter of the sixth century. Such burials were reserved for the upper echelons of society with many containing lavish grave goods. Examples include the 'Cologne princess', a richly dressed woman dating to the early sixth century, found under the floor of Cologne cathedral in 1959, who was laid to rest with pots and glass vessels containing offerings of food and drink. Similarly, a woman was laid out in her best clothes and fine gold jewellery, including a ring inscribed with the name 'Arnegundis', under the church of St-Denis, Paris, in the seventh century (Werner 1964; James 1988, 155-157). There are also several examples of objects with Christian significance being used as grave goods, both on the continent and in England. For instance the 'founder's grave' (grave 319) at Lavoye (Meuse), which can be dated to around the year 480, included a pitcher with scenes from the life of Christ on it, as well as objects that are more usually associated with 'pagan' burial such as weapons (Joffroy 1974). In England, the silver baptismal spoons from the early seventh-century Mound 1 at Sutton Hoo, Suffolk, are the most famous examples of objects with Christian significance buried in a grave; other such objects include the gold foil crosses and baptismal spoon from the 'princely' burial at Prittlewell, Essex, and the helmet with a silver cross attached to it from that at Benty Grange, Derbyshire (Bateman [1861] 1978; Carver 2005; Museum of London 2004). All of these examples of objects with Christian significance being found in graves have been interpreted as people 'hedging their bets' by displaying aspects of both the pagan (i.e. furnished burial in a barrow) and Christian (i.e. Christian symbols) religions (e.g. Carver 1998; Van de Noort 1993). However, there is no inherent reason why we should consider such burials in the seventh century to be essentially pagan in nature. In addition, the decline and disappearance of furnished burial during the late sixth and early seventh centuries is a feature not only of Anglo-Saxon England but also of burial practice on the Continent in Merovingian Gaul, where conversion to Christianity had already taken place much earlier (Halsall forthcoming 2009). We must therefore look to wider social and cultural issues than simply the conversion of the Anglo-Saxons.

The meaning of objects in Anglo-Saxon society

Direct contemporary evidence for attitudes towards the burial of personal belongings with the dead is lacking from early Anglo-Saxon England. However, later written evidence from wills reveals how people after the conversion perceived and dealt with the personal belongings of the dead. While these documents were produced in a somewhat different social context to that in which furnished burial took place, they may shed light upon how attitudes towards such objects changed across the period. Fifty-nine wills survive from the later Anglo-Saxon period, the earliest from the first decades of the ninth century but most dating from the mid-tenth to mid-eleventh centuries (Sawyer 1968; Sheehan 1963; Whitelock 1930). Although primarily concerned with the donation of land, twenty-seven surviving wills include instructions regarding the disposal of certain personal belongings after the death of the testator (Sawyer nos. S1482, S1483, S1484, S1485, S1486, S1487, S1488, S1490, S1492, S1494, S1497, S1498, S1501, S1503, S1505, S1511, S1515, S1519, S1526, S1531, S1532, S1534, S1535, S1536, S1537, S1538, S1539). These wills refer to gifts to the church, gifts to family or friends and/or the payment of heriot to the king or lord and they include references to items of jewellery, weapons, clothes, books, furniture and furnishings.[1] The wills can only be considered a partial testament to the practice of disposing of personal belongings. There must have been many more wills written than survive today and the will-makers are a small, socially restricted group of people who were primarily members of, or kin to, the royal family (Sheehan 1963; Whitelock 1930). However, the documents have been shown to be indicative of general cultural traits in late Anglo-Saxon society (ibid.), so it is likely that the attitudes towards objects displayed within these documents can be applied to wider Anglo-Saxon society. In addition, will-making seems to have been primarily an oral, performative act that took place in front of witnesses. The written aspect of making a will may well have only been of predominant concern to monastic houses, who wanted to ensure that the bequests of lands to them were not challenged at a later date. The oral act of making a will was doubtless far more widespread than the written documentation would suggest and the practice would presumably have occurred far more frequently than we have evidence for and across a wider spectrum of society.

The disposal of land and movable possessions after death had an obvious importance for the maintenance of the family's future wealth and standing (Crick 1999). However, there were also further ramifications for the donor themselves. By the late Anglo-Saxon period, it was strongly believed that the prayers of the living could influence the fate of the souls of the dead in the afterlife. Praying for the souls of the deceased was the responsibility of close family members, often women (widows, daughters; Geary 1994; Innes 2001; Van Houts 1999; 2001) but other family members too. The receiving of lands and other items of value was viewed as a gift that should be reciprocated with the counter-gift of prayers. The *Manual* of Dhuoda, written in the early 840s, exhorts her son to pray for the souls of all family members from whom he would inherit land (Innes 2001). Often among the most wealthy, the task of praying for the dead would be 'contracted-out' to religious houses, paid for by the family or through provision in the deceased's will. The evidence from the wills indicates the clear concern of the individuals who made them that prayers would be said on their behalf. The wills aim to establish long-term care for the testator's soul. Most of the wills make a least one explicit statement linking the bequests made within it to the expectation that prayers would be said for them. This is especially clear in statements concerning the giving of land. Twenty-nine wills state that land is donated to a specific religious house for the sake of the donor's soul or that of their parents or ancestors who had built up the estate(s) in the first place (S1482, S1483, S1485, S1484, S1487, S1489, S1492, S1494, S1499, S1501, S1503, S1505, S1509, S1511, S1513, S1514, S1516, S1519, S1521, S1522, S1526, S1527, S1528, S1530, S1531, S1532, S1533, S1535, S1537, S1538). Wulfgar gave the estate at Inkpen after his death and his wife's 'to the holy foundation at Kintbury to be held and enjoyed and never given away, for the soul of Wulfgar who gives it, and for Wulfric's, and for Wulfhere's who first acquired it' (S1533; Robertson 1939, 53). Many other acts recorded in the wills are also stated to be for the sake of the testator's soul, including the freeing of slaves, the distribution of food or money and the paying of food-rent to monastic houses (Beaumont 2006; Crick 2000; Sheehan 1963; Tollerton Hall 2005). In addition, some wills make arrangements for such acts to be carried out annually, on the testator's commemoration day, showing the strong link between the act of the will and its intended consequence, the remembering of the dead through prayer. For example, the will of Ceolwin, written before 905, donates land to Winchester 'for their refectory at the episcopal see, with such property as may then be fitting, on the condition that they remember the souls of her and Osmod [her husband] as to them may seem just and becoming, on his commemoration-day, which is seven

---

[1] The bequest of animals, tents, money and ships is here taken to be part of the owner's financial assets rather than their personal belongings as such and are therefore left out of the analysis.

nights before the Rogations' (S1513; Thorpe 1865, 492-3).

Much of what is recorded in the wills might be interpreted as a 'contract' between the donor and the named religious house(s) – in return for land and the wealth it generates the church would remember the individual and sing masses for them to improve the condition of the soul in the afterlife. Even where lands are given to family members, it is often only for their life, after which the estates will pass to the religious house; in the meantime, an annual food-rent or monetary gift will be provided. The benefits for all are obvious. However, the role of personal possessions in the commemoration of the dead is less clear. Only one will makes an explicit statement that the giving of personal possessions is related to caring for the donor's soul: the will of Wynflæd, a widow living in a nunnery *c*.950, describes in detail the distribution of her personal possessions to different individuals before adding that 'she makes a gift to Æthelflæd [her daughter] of everything which is unbequeathed, books and such small things, and she trusts that she will be mindful of her soul' (S1539; Whitelock 1930, 15). Given the clear link between the other acts recorded in these documents and the care for the donor's soul, it might be expected that the giving of personal possessions can be interpreted in the same way. But what specific role did people's belongings play in the commemoration of the dead? The giving of such possessions to a religious house brings only minor benefits to the recipients even when the objects are apparently of high value; they can only generate income for the monastery once, when they are sold. While the opportunity to sell an object more than once might arise – for example, Æthelstan, son of King Æthelred II, donated a drinking horn to the Old Minster, Winchester, that he had bought from the community there (S1503; Whitelock 1930, 56-57) – it is clear that many possessions were actually retained by the institution rather than being sold. When Ealdorman Brihtnoth was killed fighting the Vikings at Maldon in 991, his widow Ælfflæd donated a tapestry commemorating his military activity to Ely, along with a ring in payment of his burial fee. Ten years later, in preparing her own will (S1486; Whitelock 1930, 38-43), Ælfflæd promised the pair to that ring as part of her donation to Ely. In doing so, she not only expected that the monks would remember its significance but presumably also that they would still have the original gift. That both the original ring and the tapestry were kept for some time is indicated by the *Book of Ely*, written *c*.1170, which records the gift. Although it is not clear if Ely still possessed them in the twelfth century, the gift was still considered important enough to be worth recording at that time (Van Houts 1999, 102-3). The tapestry cannot be considered to be something or primary financial value but rather was intended to act as a reminder of Brihtnoth's deeds. The financial value of bequeathed objects was therefore only one consideration. In addition, around twice as many personal possessions are given to family members and friends as to religious houses and, unlike the estates, there is no apparent expectation that they would later go to the Church.

How, therefore, can we interpret the bequest of objects in these wills? The wider context of the documents suggest that personal belongings were implicated in the testator's strategy to ensure that they would be remembered after death. All aspects of the will were designed to ensure that the individual would be commemorated and, thus, prayed for. Although there is little in the way of explicit statements within the wills themselves, other documents indicate the commemorative aspects of bequeathing personal possessions. Making a will seems to have been part of a ritualised performance that took place as the individual neared the end of their life; it was a formal statement carried out in front of witnesses. For example, the monk Cuthbert's account of the death of Bede in the early eighth century describes how on his deathbed the latter called the priests of the monastery at Jarrow to him and distributed among them his few possessions consisting of pepper, handkerchiefs and incense (Sheehan 1963; Sherley-Price 1990). Similarly, although more showily, when Wilfrid (d.709), bishop of Ripon, realised he was nearing the end of his life, he ordered his treasurer to open the treasury at Ripon and in the presence of eight invited witnesses he divided his treasure into four portions. One portion was to go to the churches of St Peter, St Paul and St Mary in Rome for the welfare of Wilfrid's soul; a second was to be divided among the poor 'for the redemption of my soul'; a third was to allow his monastic followers to buy the friendship of kings and bishops; and the fourth was to be divided among Wilfrid's friends and supporters who had shared exile with him. Wilfrid then proceeded to travel around Northumbria repeating his will to abbots and other leaders (*Vita Sancti Wilfridi* LXIII, Colgrave 1927; Sheehan 1963).

These writings ensured that the actions of Bede and Wilfrid were remembered by a much wider audience than would have been the case for most people. Both these accounts are significant. Although it is likely that Cuthbert was emphasising Bede's poverty and generosity, the fact that he took the time on his deathbed to divide up his few possessions indicates that it was important to him who received his possessions after death, as it presumably was to the testators of the wills. These objects were carefully selected for their intended recipients. Rarely does it seem that all the individual's belongings are dealt with in the will. Studies of objects in modern western and non-western societies have indicated the important role that personal belongings can play in relationships between people over time. Objects do not merely form the background to people's lives; they are intimately involved in forming people's identities and can be tools in creating and maintaining social relationships. The object itself is of critical importance in these processes as it can carry social messages in both its design and the way it is used and can act as a stabilising and physically unchanging force in those relationships over time. Although their meaning and the messages they carry can change, the appearance and purpose of objects generally remains the same and indeed attempts are usually made to preserve important objects in their original form, for example by repairing damaged brooches. Objects therefore have a relative permanence; they can remain unchanging in appearance, in contrast to their owners who age and die and to social relationships which can dissolve or break down entirely (Kwint 1999; Hallam and Hockey 2001; see also Devlin 2007b, 41). Their longevity means that they can act as mnemonic devices, transmitting information or stories about the past from one generation to the next (Turner 1974; Richards 1992, 132; Moreland 2001, 38). Clanchy (1993) has discussed how, before charters were commonly used for recording land transactions in writing, it was usual practice to use an object to represent the transfer and act as a mnemonic for it in the future. Examples include a cup given to Durham cathedral around the time of the Conquest by Copsi, earl of Northumberland, which according to a Durham writer forty years later was preserved in the church to retain the memory of the land transaction forever, and an ivory knife deposited at Tavistock Abbey in 1096 with a note explaining that it was by this knife that William Rufus had given the abbot seisin of a manor (ibid., 38, 156). Many of the objects mentioned in the wills were apparently well-known to the recipients. As well as Offa's sword, there are the white and yellow chasubles 'which I bought in Pavia' left by Theodred, Bishop of London, to two of his friends, Odgar and another Theodred (S1526; Whitelock 1930, 2-5). Presumably both recipients would recognise the chasubles in question. Similarly, Wulfric Spott left to his goddaughter the brooch or pendant that was her grandmother's (Whitelock 1930, no. XVII; Sawyer 1968, no. 1536). In this example, it seems clear his goddaughter must have been aware of the brooch and its description seems to imply its value was related to its past ownership. The stories attached to an object might be more valuable than the thing itself, enhancing the current owner's status. Several wills refer to objects known to have been associated with other people, such as 'the sword which belonged to King Offa' left by the Ætheling Æthelstan to his brother Edmund (S1503; Whitelock 1930, 58-59). As Offa died in 796, this sword would have been around 220 years old. In many respects, it does not matter if the sword in question really had been Offa's; the fact that it was believed to have been would have given it special significance and there would have been stories attached to it. It was evidently well known as Offa's sword: most of the other swords left by Æthelstan are identified by their physical appearance. As objects are implicated in social relationships between people, through being involved in rituals, display and gift-giving, they can act as physical reminders of those relationships at the same time as creating and maintaining them.

Objects are not just important for maintaining social relationships but can act as mnemonics for the lives of their owners, especially at critical times where people perceive themselves as nearing the end of their lives (Battaglia 1992; Hoskins 1998; Küchler 1987; Radley 1990; Taylor 1993; Unruh 1983; Weiner 1992; Weiss 1997; see also Csikszentmihalyi and Rochberg-Halton 1981; Devlin 2007a, 21-25 for full discussion). In such situations, personal belongings can provide a framework in which people take stock of their lives, providing a focus for remembering the past and sharing those memories with family members, with the object in question placed at the centre of a narrative about what the owner wishes people to know about their lives. In modern societies, individual people may actively try to shape how people will remember them after their death by bequeathing certain possessions to friends and relatives who will understand their significance (Unruh 1983). Such objects can become 'sacred symbols', representing aspects of the deceased's life that are important to their surviving relatives (Unruh 1983). Objects can be an important means of managing grief, providing a focus for remembrance. The preservation of some of the deceased's belongings aids the retention of memories of aspects of the deceased's identity. The Anglo-Saxon wills may represent evidence of a similar process, with people choosing certain possessions to leave to family, friends or religious houses with which they had been closely associated in their lifetime to act as a physical reminder of the owner and shape how they would be remembered. For family and friends, preserving such 'sacred symbols' and the memories that go with them can be an important way in which the bereaved deal with feelings of grief and loss (Ash 1996; Hallam and Hockey 2001; Unruh 1983, 347).

It can be argued therefore that the bequest of personal belongings in Anglo-Saxon wills was intended to secure prayers for the testators in a very specific way, acting as physical reminders of the deceased and the need to pray for them. Many of the objects were mundane items, such as clothing and furniture, that would enable reminders of the dead to be encountered in everyday life. Unlike other aspects of the wills, the bequest of objects relied upon individual memories of the deceased and their personality and identity to encourage people to pray for them. The close relationship between objects and identity that is argued to exist for interment with grave goods can therefore be seen to continue beyond the eighth century and the end of widespread furnished burial.

The end of furnished burial

We can see therefore that personal possessions can be very closely associated with the lives and personalities of their owners, acting as reminders of events from the past and being used as a focus for stories that their owners consider to be important aspects of their own characters. If anything, this association between object and owner is so strong that it not only continues but intensifies after the person's death, with the object acting as a reminder of the deceased and particular aspects of their life. This association between objects and memories of the past may provide us with an explanation of how the Anglo-Saxons dealt with the possessions of deceased loved ones, both before and after the conversion to Christianity. Whether buried in the grave with their owner or willed to the living, the ways that objects were disposed of reveal how people related to the dead and their memories during the Anglo-Saxon period. Throughout the period, the disposal of the deceased's personal possessions occurred in a highly ritualised manner and at a time of intense emotions. The end of furnished burial represents a major change in the way that people dealt with the possessions of their loved ones. Rather than selected items being chosen, most likely by the mourners, to accompany the deceased in the grave, important objects were now distributed at the will of their owners to particular family members and churches. This can be related to two major changes that took place during this period: a change in the relationship between the living and the dead, particularly with regard to how the dead were remembered, and a related change in the perception of ownership of objects.

The objects laid out in the grave with the deceased can be shown to create a tableau that was designed to present a particular image of them to the people at the funeral (Halsall 1998; 2003). This image is created by the deceased's family through the careful selection of objects from a limited range of choices, each with a meaning that was fully understood by contemporaries. These meanings could have significance at both the local level and more generally in Anglo-Saxon society so that for instance burial with weapons might represent general attributes of military prowess, youthfulness, strength and other 'warrior' attributes that would be recognised by people all over the country, while at the same time representing particular characteristics that were important among the people of the region, such as being of a particular ethnic group. This image presented in the grave was very much an idealised one, drawing upon a set of standard 'rules' of appropriate funeral behaviour (Devlin 2007a, 34-37), which would also have extended beyond the funerary ritual itself to encompass archaeologically invisible practices and appropriate behaviours. These rules provided a means of dealing with grief at the loss of a loved one by imposing social constraints on behaviour at a time when normal life is suspended and strong emotions are in play. They also provided a means of linking the funerals of the dead, so that each burial called to mind ones that had occurred before (Halsall 2003). By creating a new identity for the deceased person and linking them into the 'community' of the dead, the living were able to separate themselves from the dead both emotionally and socially, thus beginning the process of 'moving on' (Devlin 2007a). The funeral was therefore part of a coping strategy for both the family of the deceased and the wider community and the careful selection and burial of certain of their belongings played an important part in this process.

The decision to no longer inter the dead with their belongings therefore represents a major upheaval in burial practices, albeit one that occurred over a long period of time. This was a decision that was presumably at first made on an individual basis, with some people in the seventh and early eighth centuries being buried in the traditional manner and others not. For one thing, the wills indicate that individual people were increasingly becoming involved in choosing what happened to their belongings after their death, rather than this being left to their survivors. This might be related to changes in land ownership and control at the same time, with the pattern of inheritance changing from land being passed down among kin to the idea that some estates could be willed to the church by individuals. The written evidence indicates that personal belongings were still closely linked to the deceased's identity, especially the aspects of their identity that were to be remembered after their death. However, the decision not to bury them with the body but to preserve them among people who had known their owner suggests that the timescale for memory and the manipulation of identity was changing. When objects are buried in the grave, they create an image of the deceased which is transitory in duration (cf., Halsall 1998; 2003); once the grave is filled in that image can no longer be manipulated and is preserved only within the memory of those who witnessed it. By keeping objects out of the grave, in the hands of family and friends, those objects can continue to act as a mnemonic for their owners for as long as stories attached to them endure. While the interment of objects within the grave can be seen as a way of 'finishing' memories of the dead and separating them from the living, the practice of preserving objects among people who had known the deceased in life indicates the ending of this desire to separate the living from the dead. In the later Anglo-Saxon period, the dead were kept among the living, buried in churchyards within towns and villages, with their possessions serving to bring them into people's thoughts.

Conclusion

Throughout the Anglo-Saxon period, personal belongings were of great importance in the ways that people dealt with death and memories of the dead. However, the conversion to Christianity led to a reinterpretation of the relationship between objects, identity and the memory of the dead. The developing concern for the fate of the soul meant that individual people were more concerned about shaping their own identity after death, through bequests, than they had been before the conversion. Remembrance of the dead also became a much longer term commitment, with memories intended to last for all time. It is notable though that many of the same objects are found in both graves and wills, indicating that the creation of an idealised identity for the dead based on important cultural attributes, such as symbols of warrior status, continued. This may have been of greater concern for people who could not depend upon family members to pray for them. The disparity in reference to objects between the wills of men and women has already been commented upon (Beaumont 2006; Crick 1999): the bequest of objects occurs far more frequently in women's wills than in men's. This has already been suggested (Tollerton Hall 2005, 207) to be the result of men being more likely to leave a surviving spouse than women. Men could rely upon their widows to ensure they were remembered (cf., Van Houts 1999) while women were more likely to need to make their own provision. The family therefore remains important in shaping commemoration of the dead throughout the Anglo-Saxon period. However, the aims and methods change over time. Although the surviving wills are from a later date than the end of furnished burial, they contain important evidence about changes in attitudes towards memory and objects which shed light upon the observed changes in the archaeological record.

Acknowledgements

This paper is partly based on research conducted for my doctoral degree at the Centre for Medieval Studies, University of York, which was funded by the Arts and Humanities Research Council and the British Federation of Women Graduates Charitable Foundation. My thanks go to Katy Cubitt, Guy Halsall and Caroline Holas-Clark for comments on this paper.

Bibliography

Arnold, C. 1980. 'Wealth and social structure: a matter of life and death', in P. Rahtz, T. Dickinson and L. Watts (eds.), *Anglo-Saxon Cemeteries 1979*, B.A.R., British Series, 82 (Oxford): 81-140

Ash, J. 1996. 'Memory and objects', in P. Kirkham (ed.), *The Gendered Object*, Manchester University Press (Manchester): 219-224

Bateman, T. [1861] 1978. *Ten Years' Diggings in Celtic and Saxon Grave Hills: in the Counties of Derby, Stafford and York, from 1848-1858*, Moorland Reprints (Buxton)

Battaglia, D. 1992. 'The body in the gift: memory and forgetting in Sabarl mortuary exchange', *American Ethnologist*, 19 (1): 3-18

Beaumont, N. 2006. *Mothers, mothering and motherhood in Late Anglo-Saxon England*, unpublished Ph.D. dissertation, University of York

[Bede] 1990. *Ecclesiastical History of the English People*, transl. L. Sherley-Price, revised by R.E. Latham, Penguin (London)

Boddington, A. 1990. 'Models of burial, settlement and worship: the Final Phase reviewed', in E. Southworth (ed.), *Anglo-Saxon Cemeteries: a Reappraisal*, Alan Sutton Publishers Ltd (Stroud): 177-199

Bullough, D. 1981. 'Burial, community and belief in the early medieval west', in C.P. Wormald, D. Bullough and R. Collins (eds.), *Ideal and Reality in Frankish and Anglo-Saxon Society*, Basil Blackwell (Oxford): 177-201

Carver, M.O.H. 1998. *Sutton Hoo. Burial Ground of Kings?*, British Museum Press (London)

Carver, M.O.H. 2005. *Sutton Hoo: a Princely Burial Ground and its Context*, British Museum Press (London)

Clanchy, M.T. 1993. *From Memory to Written Record. England 1066-1307*, Blackwell (Oxford)

Colgrave, B. (transl.) 1927. *The Life of Bishop Wilfrid*, Cambridge University Press (Cambridge)

Crawford, S. 1993. 'Children, death and the afterlife in Anglo-Saxon England', in W. Filmer-Sankey (ed.), *Anglo-Saxon Studies in Archaeology and History*, 6, Oxford University Committee for Archaeology (Oxford): 83-91

Crawford, S. 1999. *Childhood in Anglo-Saxon England*, Sutton Publishing Ltd (Stroud)

Crawford, S. 2000. 'Children, grave goods and social status in Early Anglo-Saxon England', in J.S. Derevenski (ed.), *Children and Material Culture*, Routledge (London and New York): 169-179

Crick, J. 1999. 'Women, posthumous benefaction and family strategy in pre-Conquest England', *Journal of British Studies*, 38: 399-422

Crick, J. 2000. 'Posthumous obligation and family identity', in W.O. Frazer and A. Tyrrell (eds.), *Social Identity in Early Medieval Britain*, Leicester University Press (London and New York): 193-208

Csikszentmihalyi, M. and Rochberg-Halton, E. 1981. *The Meaning of Things. Domestic Symbols and the Self*, Cambridge University Press (Cambridge)

Devlin, Z.L. 2007a. *Remembering the Dead in Anglo-Saxon England: Memory Theory in Archaeology and History*, B.A.R., British Series, 446 (Oxford)

Devlin, Z.L. 2007b. 'Social memory, material culture and community identity in early medieval mortuary practices', in S. Semple and H. Williams (eds.), *Anglo-Saxon Studies in Archaeology and History*, 14, Oxford University Committee for Archaeology (Oxford): 38-46

Down, A. and Welch, M. 1990. *Chichester Excavations 7: Apple Down and the Mardens*, Chichester District Council (Chichester)

Effros, B. 1997. 'Beyond cemetery walls: early medieval funerary topography and Christian salvation', *Early Medieval Europe*, 6 (1): 1-23

Effros, B. 2002. *Caring for Body and Soul. Burial and the Afterlife in the Merovingian World*, Pennsylvania State University Press (Philadelphia)

Evison, V. 1956. 'An Anglo-Saxon cemetery at Holborough, Kent', *Archaeologia Cantiana*, 70: 84-141

Faull, M.L. 1976. 'The location and relationship of the Sancton Anglo-Saxon cemeteries', *Antiquaries Journal*, 56: 227-233

Geake, H. 1992. 'Burial practices in seventh- and eighth-century England', in M.O.H. Carver (ed.), *The Age of Sutton Hoo. The Seventh Century in North-western Europe*, The Boydell Press (Woodbridge): 83-94

Geake, H. 1997. *The Use of Grave-Goods in Conversion Period England, c.600-c.850*, B.A.R., British Series, 261 (Oxford)

Geary, P. 1994 *Phantoms of Remembrance. Memory and Oblivion at the End of the First Millennium*, Princeton University Press (Princeton)

Gittos, H. 2002. 'Creating the sacred: Anglo-Saxon rites for consecrating cemeteries', in S. Lucy & A. Reynolds (eds.), *Burial in Early Medieval England and Wales*, Society for Medieval Archaeology (London): 195-208

Hadley, D.M. 2001. *Death in Medieval England. An Archaeology*, Tempus Publishing Ltd (Stroud)

Hadley, D.M. and Moore, J.M. 1998. ''Death makes the man'? Burial rite and the construction of masculinities in the early middle ages', in D.M. Hadley (ed.), *Masculinity in Medieval Europe*: 21-38

Hallam, E. and Hockey, J. 2001. *Death, Memory and Material Culture*, Berg (Oxford and New York)

Halsall, G. 1998. 'Burial, ritual and Merovingian society', in J. Hill and M. Swan (eds.), *The Community, the Family and the Saint. Patterns of Power in Early Medieval Europe*, Selected Proceedings of the International Medieval Congress, University of Leeds, 1994 and 1995, Brepols (Turnhout): 325-338

Halsall, G. 2000. 'The Viking presence in England. The burial evidence reconsidered', in D. Hadley and J. Richards (eds.), *Cultures in Contact: Scandinavian Settlement in England in the Ninth and Tenth Centuries*, Brepols (Turnhout): 295-310

Halsall, G. 2003. 'Burial writes: graves, "texts" and time in early Merovingian northern Gaul', in J. Jarnut and M. Wemhoff (eds.), *Erinnerungskultur im Bestattungsritual. Archäologisch-Historisches Forum*, Wilhelm Fink Verlag (Munich): 61-74

Halsall, G. forthcoming 2009. 'Examining the Christianization of the region of Metz from archaeological sources (5th-7th Centuries): problems, possibilities and implications for Anglo-Saxon England', in *id.*, *Cemeteries and Society in Merovingian Gaul: Selected Studies in Archaeology and History, 1992-2008*, E.J. Brill (Leiden)

Härke, H. 1989a. 'Early Saxon weapon burials: frequencies, distributions and weapons combinations', in S.C. Hawkes (ed.), *Weapons and Warfare in Anglo-Saxon England*, Oxford University Committee for Archaeology (Oxford): 49-61

Härke, H. 1989b. 'Knives in early Anglo-Saxon burials: blade length and age at death', *Medieval Archaeology*, 33: 144-148

Härke, H. 1990. 'Warrior graves? The background of the Anglo-Saxon weapon burial rite', *Past and Present*, 126: 22-43

Härke, H. 1992. 'Changing symbols in a changing society: The Anglo-Saxon weapon burial rite in the seventh century', in M.O.H. Carver (ed.), *The Age of Sutton Hoo*, Boydell Press (Woodbridge): 149-165

Härke, H. 1997. 'Material culture as myth: weapons in Anglo-Saxon graves', in C. Kjeld Jensen and K. Høilund Nielsen (eds.), *Burial and Society. The Chronological and Social Analysis of Archaeological Burial Data*, Aarhus University Press (Aarhus): 119-127

Hines, J. 1992. 'The seriation and chronology of Anglian English women's graves: a critical assessment', in L. Jørgensen (ed.), *Chronological Studies of Anglo-Saxon England, Lombard Italy and Vendel Period Sweden*, University of Copenhagen Institute of Prehistoric and Classical Archaeology, Arkæologiske Skrifter, 5 (Copenhagen): 50-80

Hines, J. 1994. 'The becoming of the English: identity, material culture and language in early Anglo-Saxon England', in W. Filmer-Sankey and D. Griffiths (eds.), *Anglo-Saxon Studies in Archaeology and History*, 7, Oxford University Committee for Archaeology (Oxford): 49-59

Hogarth, A.C. 1973. 'Structural features in Anglo-Saxon graves', *Archaeological Journal*, 130: 104-119

Hoggett, R. 2007. 'Charting conversion: burial as a barometer of belief?', in S. Semple and H. Williams (eds.), *Anglo-Saxon Studies in Archaeology and History*, 14, Oxford University Committee for Archaeology (Oxford): 29-37

Hoskins, J. 1998. *Biographical Objects. How Things Tell the Stories of People's Lives*, Routledge (London & New York)

Hyslop, M. 1963. 'Two Anglo-Saxon cemeteries at Chamberlains Barn, Leighton Buzzard, Bedfordshire', *Archaeological Journal*, 120: 161-200

Innes, M. 2001.'Keeping it in the family: women and aristocratic memory, 700-1200', in E.M.C. Van Houts (ed.) *Medieval Memories. Men, Women and the Past, 700-1300*, Pearson Education Ltd (Harlow): 17-35

James, E. 1988. *The Franks*, Blackwell (Oxford and New York)

James, E. 1989. 'Burial and status in the early medieval West', *Transactions of the Royal Historical Society*, 5th series, 29: 23-40

Joffroy, R. 1974. *Le Cimetière de Lavoye (Meuse)*, A. & J. Picard (Paris)

Küchler, S. 1987. 'Malangan: art and memory in a Melanesian society', *Man*, 22: 238-255

Kwint, M. 1999. 'Introduction: the physical past', in M. Kwint, C. Breward and J. Aynsley (eds.), *Material Memories. Design and Evocation*, Berg (Oxford and New York): 1-16

Leeds, E.T. 1913. *The Archaeology of the Anglo-Saxon Settlements*, Clarendon Press (Oxford)

Lethbridge, T.C. 1931. *Recent Excavations in Anglo-Saxon Cemeteries in Cambridgeshire and Suffolk*, Cambridge Antiquarian Society Quarto Publications, New Series, 3, Bowes and Bowes

Lethbridge, T.C. 1936. *A Cemetery at Shudy Camps, Cambridgeshire. Report of the Excavation of a Cemetery of the Christian Anglo-Saxon Period in 1933*, Cambridge Antiquarian Society Quarto Publications, New Series, 5, Bowes and Bowes

Lucy, S. 1994. 'Children in early medieval cemeteries', *Archaeological Review from Cambridge*, 13 (2): 21-34

Lucy, S. 1997. 'Housewives, warriors and slaves? Sex and gender in Anglo-Saxon burials', in J. Moore and E. Scott (eds.), *Invisible People and Processes: Writing Gender and Childhood into European Archaeology*, Leicester University Press (London and New York): 150-168

Malim, T. and Hines, J. 1998. *The Anglo-Saxon Cemetery at Edix Hill (Barrington A), Cambridgeshire*, Council for British Archaeology Research Report, 112 (York)

Meaney, A.L. and Hawkes, S.C. 1970. *Two Anglo-Saxon Cemeteries at Winnall, Winchester, Hampshire*, Society for Medieval Archaeology Monograph Series, 4 (London)

Moreland, J. 2001. *Archaeology and Text*, Gerald Duckworth and Co Ltd (London)

Morris, R. 1983. *The Church in British Archaeology*, Council for British Archaeology, Research Report, 47 (London)

Museum of London, 2004. *The Prittlewell Prince. The Discovery of a Rich Anglo-Saxon Burial in Essex*, Museum of London Archaeology Service (London)

Owen-Crocker, G.R. 2004. *Dress in Anglo-Saxon England*, Boydell Press (Woodbridge)

Paxton, F.S. 1990. *Christianizing Death. The Creation of a Ritual Process in Early Medieval Europe*, Cornell University Press (Ithaca & London)

Radley, A. 1990. 'Artefacts, memory and a sense of the past', in D. Middleton and D. Edwards (eds.), *Collective Remembering*, Sage Publications (London): 46-59

Richards, J.D. 1992. 'Anglo-Saxon symbolism', in M.O.H. Carver (ed.), *The Age of Sutton Hoo. The Seventh Century in North-western Europe*, The Boydell Press (Woodbridge): 131-148

Robertson, A.J. 1939. *Anglo-Saxon Charters*, Cambridge University Press

Sawyer, P.H. 1968. *Anglo-Saxon Charters: An Annotated List and Bibliography*, Royal Historical Society (London)

Sheehan, M. 1963. *The Will in Medieval England. From the Conversion of the Anglo-Saxons to the End of the Thirteenth Century*, Pontifical Institute of Medieval Studies (Toronto)

Sherley-Price, L. 1990. 'Cuthbert's *Letter on the illness and death of the Venerable Bede, the priest*', in *Bede's Ecclesiastical History of the English People*, transl. L. Sherley-Price, revised by R.E. Latham, Penguin (London): 357-360

Stoodley, N. 1999. *The Spindle and the Spear. A Critical Enquiry into the Construction and Meaning of Gender in the Early Anglo-Saxon Burial Rite*, B.A.R., British Series, 288

Taylor, A.C. 1993. 'Remembering to forget: identity, mourning and memory among the Jivaro', *Man*, New Series, 28 (4): 653-678

Thorpe, B. 1865. *Diplomatarium Anglicum Aevi Saxonici. A Collection of English Charters From the Reign of King Æthelberht of Kent, AD DC.V. to that of William the Conqueror*, Macmillan and Co (London)

Tollerton Hall, L. 2005. *Wills and will-making in Late Anglo-Saxon England*, unpublished Ph.D. dissertation, University of York

Turner, V. 1974. *Dramas, Fields and Metaphors: Symbolic Action in Human Society*, Cornell University Press (Ithaca & London)

Unruh, D.R. 1983. 'Death and personal history: strategies of identity preservation', *Social Problems*, 30 (3): 340-351

Van de Noort, R. 1993. 'The context of early medieval barrows in western Europe', *Antiquity*, 67: 66-73

Van Houts, E.M.C. 1999. *Memory and Gender in Medieval Europe, 900-1200*, Macmillan Press Ltd (London)

Van Houts, E.M.C. 2001. 'Introduction. Medieval memories', in E.M.C. Van Houts (ed.), *Medieval*

Memories. Men, Women and the Past, 700-1300, Pearson Education Ltd (Harlow), 1-16

Weiner, A.B. 1992. *Inalienable Possessions: the Paradox of Keeping-While-Giving*, University of California Press (Berkeley, Los Angeles, Oxford)

Weiss, B. 1997. 'Forgetting your dead: alienable and inalienable objects in northwest Tanzania', *Anthropological Quarterly*, 70: 164-172

Werner, J. 1964. 'Frankish royal tombs in the cathedrals of Cologne and St-Denis', *Antiquity*, 38: 201-16

Whitelock, D. (ed. and transl.) 1930. *Anglo-Saxon Wills*, Cambridge University Press (Cambridge)

Williams, H. 2003. 'Material culture as memory: combs and cremation in early medieval Britain', *Early Medieval Europe*, 12: 89-128

Williams, H. 2007. 'Transforming body and soul: toilet implements in early Anglo-Saxon graves', in S. Semple and H. Williams (eds.), *Anglo-Saxon Studies in Archaeology and History*, 14, Oxford University Committee for Archaeology (Oxford): 66-91

Young, B.K. 1975. *Merovingian funeral rites and the evolution of Christianity: a study in the historical interpretation of archaeological material*, University of Pennsylvania PhD Dissertation (Ann Arbor)

Young, B.K. 1977. 'Paganisme, christianisme et rites funéraires mérovingiens', *Archéologie Médiévale*, 7: 5-81

Zadora Rio, E. 2003. 'The making of churchyards and parish territories in the early-medieval landscape of France and England in the 7th-12th centuries: A reconsideration', *Medieval Archaeology*, 47: 1-19

Sculpture and lordship in Late Saxon Suffolk: the evidence of Ixworth

Michael F. Reed

Historiography and methodology

For much of the twentieth century, the study of England's pre-Conquest sculpture was largely typological in nature. Shaped principally by Collingwood, initial research privileged style-analysis and chronology and promoted a linear evolutionary model with Northumbria as its apparent nucleus (cf., Collingwood 1927)[1]. A tentative movement toward contextualization and interpretation of Anglo-Saxon sculpture, in relative concurrence with contemporaneous Scottish material, emerged in the first half of the twentieth century and is demonstrated by Allen and Anderson's *The Early Christian Monuments of Scotland* (1903) and Collingwood's *Northumbrian Crosses of the Pre-Norman Age* (1927). These vast typological studies influenced later scholars of Insular sculpture, including Nash-Williams and Henry. Nash-Williams' *The Early Christian Monuments of Wales* (1950) and much of Henry's work, including *Irish Art in the Early Christian Period* (1940) and *Irish High Crosses* (1964), replicate the national scope of earlier research while exploring the contexts for sculptural patronage, production and use more fully than their predecessors (Henry 1940, 1-10; Henry 1964, 1-4; Nash-Williams 1950, 1-5).

By the 1970s, the study of Insular sculpture was well-developed within the growing field of Medieval Studies[2], and several scholars (Cramp, Bailey and Lang) displayed particular interest in Anglo-Scandinavian material. Building upon Collingwood's work, Cramp, Bailey and Lang undertook important projects which, collectively, brought attention, interest and significance to the corpus of Anglo-Scandinavian sculpture (cf., Bailey 1978; 1980; Cramp 1982; and Lang 1973). However, unlike earlier assessments of England's pre-Norman stonework, Cramp, Bailey and Lang approached stone monuments as evidence of social history. Explicit in their studies is the importance of iconographic analysis, something which had rarely been discussed in any substantive way in the earlier typological assessments.

This paper builds on the methodology advanced by Cramp, Bailey and Lang. It includes iconographic readings but also employs textual (including onomastic) and other forms of material evidence. It is hoped that this approach will stimulate generation of an integrated social history of Late Saxon Suffolk and demonstrate the viability of interdisciplinary methodology to Anglo-Saxon sculptural studies.

Anglo-Saxon lordship and patronage

In pre-Conquest East Anglia, lordship and patronage were complex, interrelated processes. Benefaction of architecture and prestige objects, whether small or of monumental scale, demanded substantial wealth. Resultant commissions displayed patrons' affluence and conveyed messages of power and authority (Fleming 2001, 12-13). Influenced by earlier traditions of gift-giving, the lord's role as a 'giver-of-gifts' coalesced into the dual roles of '*seigneur*' and patron. Benefaction and display of wealth proclaimed and reaffirmed lordly status; stone sculpture played an important role in that process, serving as a tangible, permanent symbol of one's station.

Archaeological and literary evidence demonstrates that socio-political relationships in Anglo-Saxon England were regulated and maintained principally through the exchange of gifts (cf., Härke 2000, 377-399). In addition to religious patronage, gift-giving is evidenced by weapon-burial, river deposition, heroic poetry, law codes, wills and letters (ibid., 377). This evidence spans the entire Anglo-Saxon period (*circa* late fifth to mid-eleventh century): the rite of weapon-burial is of fifth- to eighth-century date (Geake 1992, 83-86); heroic poetry (*Beowulf*, for example) has been variously assigned to the eighth or tenth centuries, though such poems often preserve earlier material; and the laws pertaining to *heriot* (a form of death tax) and wills date to the ninth to eleventh centuries (Härke 2000, 377-378).[3] Härke has demonstrated, convincingly, that the various dates ascribed to these evidential categories are attributable to the nature of the sources themselves; therefore they cannot be interpreted as accurate delimiters of the practices they reflect or describe (ibid., 378). For example, though the tradition of weapon-burial ceases *circa* 700, this can be interpreted in the context of the general decline in grave-good deposition (ibid.). It is also apparent that heroic poetry could not have been

---

[1] Hawkes (2007) has recently discussed Collingwood's role in the study of Anglo-Saxon sculpture and the material's methodological complexity *vis à vis* archaeology and art history.

[2] The label 'Medieval Studies' is used cautiously with reference to the 1970s. The formation of Medieval Studies departments is generally associated with the late 1970s to mid 1980s. Prior to this period, medieval research was generally conducted in those departments which would become the 'parents' of Medieval Studies (including languages, History and Archaeology). In the 1970s, most Insular sculptural research was undertaken by archaeologists.

[3] 'Between the ninth and eleventh centuries, the gift (or return) of weapons from follower to lord became formalized as *heriot*, and enshrined in law. The secular laws of King Cnut (issued probably between AD 1020 and 1023) stipulated that any nobleman of the rank of thegn or above had to provide for weapons and money to be given on the occasion of his own death to the king. This *heriot* was graded by rank, and differentiated by region' (Härke 2000, 382). For a discussion of early Anglo-Saxon wills, see Sheehan (1963, 23). For a discussion of later Anglo-Saxon wills, see Tollerton-Hall (2005, throughout).

transcribed prior to the reintroduction of literacy into England beginning in the seventh century, nor could the existence and oral tradition of poetry, together with other practices including gift-giving and looting, be dismissed before that date (ibid.). While the earliest Anglo-Saxon wills are attributable to the ninth century, the notion of inheritance predates this period (heirloom, for example, is identified as an existing practice in the seventh-century laws of Æthelberht of Kent, c.602-603; ibid.). Despite such profound changes in Anglo-Saxon society, Härke's hypothesis that the various forms of gift-giving between the seventh and ninth centuries are broadly contemporary seems justified.

In the ninth century, land became an increasingly important commodity in the gift-centred society of Anglo-Saxon England. In addition to gifts of money and material goods, loans of land were granted to retainers in exchange for faithful service. Through such service, each generation acquired its use of land (Abels 1988, 44). A late ninth-century diploma recounts this process:

> During his lifetime the aforementioned Cenwald instructed that, if his son Census should serve the king or enter his following, he should be the lord of this land as long as he lived (quoted ibid.).

The commissioners of the *Domesday* inquest had assumed that during the reign of Edward the Elder (899-925), the Saxon kingdoms had been organized into *mansiones* or estates (Stenton 1943; 1989, 480). Before the end of the tenth century, the phrase '*heafod botl*' ('chief dwelling') was employed as a descriptor not only of a lord's residence, but also of those adjacent lands which supported his household (ibid.). By the mid-eleventh century, tenurial lords might possess multi-*vill* ('village') *sokes* ('estates') comprising a manorial centre and numerous *berewicks* and *sokelands* (dependencies of a *soke*; Hadley 2000, 167).

Lords and sculpture

While commissioning stone sculpture certainly demonstrated affluence and power (ecclesiastical, secular or both) in Anglo-Saxon society, other reasons for patronizing sculptors are largely conjectural. Later evidence is potentially useful in this instance, especially Hill's tripartite theory of monastic patronage. In his study of benefaction and Cistercian foundations in twelfth-century England, Hill proposes three reasons for monastic patronage by lay elites: (1) to assuage guilt for evil deeds; (2) to demonstrate elites' 'duty' in a gift-giving society; and (3) to express lay spirituality ([1968] 1984, 175-177). Cownie concurs with Hill's concept of religious patronage as gift-giving, suggesting that in late eleventh-century England, such patronage was recognized as philanthropy (1998, 7); she also notes that the gift was 'never a simple exchange of goods' (ibid., 26).[4] Thus, in a monastic context for example, a patron would donate or bequeath to the church, and the religious community would preserve the *memoria* of the deceased through prayer – a principal monastic function (ibid., 6). Lay patronage of religious houses can also be interpreted as a societal gift: the *caritas* of the patron inspires emulation, generating a cycle of benefaction which reinforces the status of the church and its tenets and models appropriate Christian behaviour, especially amongst elites.

Lordship and sculpture in Late Saxon Ixworth, Sf.

Ixworth is located in northwestern Suffolk, approximately ten km northeast of Bury St Edmunds. In the tenth and eleventh centuries, Suffolk, Norfolk and Lincolnshire, together with much of the land which shared their borders, were among the wealthiest counties in England. This wealth was attributable to intensified agriculture. Danish settlers exploited the region's rich soil and temperate climate, bringing much of the region under cultivation, including areas which had never been farmed: the marsh of Lincolnshire, the forests of northwest Nottinghamshire and the flat lands along the Norfolk broads (Stenton 1943, 513).

It is likely that these East Anglian counties had also been affluent earlier in the Anglo-Saxon period. This is seemingly confirmed in Suffolk by archaeological evidence from Ixworth. Two gold rings, two silver rings, a gold earring and a gilt bronze ring (all probably of seventh- to eighth-century date) were recovered in or near St Mary's churchyard in the 1850s (Suffolk SMR OS Card TL97SW22). Furthermore, a gold, jewelled disc brooch, and a gold pendent cross decorated with *cloisonné* garnet-work, together with a number of iron staples (presumably coffin-fittings), were removed from an elite grave at Stanton, Ixworth, in 1856 (MacGregor and Bolick 1993, 78, 159). The pendent cross is comparable in both form and size to the pectoral cross of St Cuthbert. Such finds suggest that considerable wealth was concentrated near Ixworth in the Middle Saxon period.[5] The pendent cross perhaps suggests an elite ecclesiastical presence also, though contemporaneous stone sculpture, often associated with such contexts, has not been identified.

Following Danish settlement, Ixworth obviously grew in both size and importance, evidenced by the existence of Ixworth Thorpe, a village northwest of Ixworth. The Old Norse word '*þorp*' is usually interpreted as an indicator of secondary settlement, either a dependency of a larger estate or an instance of subsequent exploitation of marginal land (Cameron 1977, 139, 141; Nenk, Margeson

---

[4] Huneberc's eighth-century discussion concerning the erection of crosses on nobles' estates also supports Hills' theory that religious patronage can be understood as an elite 'duty' in a gift-giving society; it also implies that this interpretation of patronage antedates the eleventh/twelfth century (see Dodwell 1982, 111).

[5] Based on this author's research, Anglo-Saxon 'archaeology' at Ixworth was primarily associated with the nineteenth century (cf., Smith [1907] 1975, 337). Recent finds have been reported by metal-detectorists and documented by the *PAS* (*Portable Antiquities Scheme*).

and Hurley 1994, 253). Though this onomastic evidence suggests that Ixworth was an important centre *circa* ninth to eleventh centuries, little is known of its settlement geography. *Domesday* records that *'Aki'* (an ON appellation) held Ixworth as a manor *tempore Regis Edwardi* (1042-1066).[6] It is possible that a similar organization of land holdings existed in Ixworth in the ninth and tenth centuries, especially since the settlement had been large enough to warrant the foundation of a dependent village prior to the completion of *Domesday*. If such an organization continued into the Late Saxon period, then it is possible that one or more manors existed in Ixworth *circa* ninth-eleventh centuries, and by the nature of manorial organization, probably possessed considerable wealth.

Like the parish's settlement geography, Ixworth's early ecclesiastical history is also unclear. Based on the discovery of two eleventh-century grave-slab fragments beneath the floor of St Mary's Church in Ixworth, it is evident that the site had an ecclesiastical function (cemetery, church or both) in the Viking Age.[7] As posited above, it is also possible that Anglo-Saxon ecclesiastical use predated this foundation, suggested by interment and by funerary deposition of the *cloisonné* pendent cross. Thus, it is tentatively hypothesized that Danish settlement at Ixworth disrupted established patterns of religious authority, precipitating the foundation of a manorial church by a wealthy land-owner.

Selected finds' record
i) *Parts of coffin-lids or grave-covers*, Moyse's Hall Museum, Bury St Edmunds, no. 1977.946, *circa* eleventh century (Figs. 1-2)

Ixworth 1A. Courtesy Moyse's Hall Museum. ©Michael F. Reed, 2006

Ixworth 1A is a coffin-lid or grave-cover that has been cut down for secondary use, possibly in an architectural context.[8] The surviving portion is the wider end of a tapered slab, the horizontal angles of which are chamfered. The principal element in the stone's decorative programme is a centrally-placed cruciform with wedge-shaped arms (type B6; Cramp 1984, xvi), the shaft of which bisects the slab and terminates in a semi-circular motif. In the interstices formed by the convergence of the cross-arms and -shaft are two recessed panels of four-cord plaitwork, though no attempt has been made by the sculptor to emphasize cord-layering at crossing points.

Ixworth 1B. Courtesy Moyse's Hall Museum. ©Michael F. Reed, 2006.

Ixworth 1B is also a coffin-lid or grave-cover that has been recut for secondary use, again, possibly in an architectural context.[9] The surviving fragment is one end

---

[6] 'Aki held Ixworth as a manor TRE with 3 carucates of land. Then as now 2 bordars. Then 5 slaves, now 2. Then as now 3 ploughs in demesne. 1 mill. 20 acres of meadow. Then 2 horses, now 1. Then as now 5 head of cattle. Then 40 pigs, now 22. Then 8 sheep, now 92; 3 arpents of vines. 1 park. Then it was worth 80s., now £6. In the same place 25 free men by commendation [held] 2½ carucates of land. Then 5 ploughs, now 4½; 4 acres of meadow. Then as now worth 20s. St Edmund had the sake and soke over the whole Hundred. In the same place 5 free men by commendation [held] 1 carucate of land and 80 acres. Then 5 ploughs, now 2; 3 acres of meadow. Then it was worth 30s., now 20s. A church with 80 acres of free land and 1 plough and 1 acre of meadow worth 5s. The whole is 2 leagues long and 6 furlongs broad. 22¾d. in geld'. '*Achi p mań.t.r.e.III.car terræ.femp.II.bord.Tć.v.feru.m.II.femp.III.car in dńio.&.I.mol.⁊ XX.ać pti.Tć.II.runc.modo.I.Sép.V.ań.Tć.XL.porc.modo.XX.II.Tć.VIII.oús.modo LXXXX.II.⁊ III.arpenni uineæ.& un parc.Tć ual.LXXX. fol.modo.VI.lib.In eadé.XXV.libi hoes.com.II.car.& dina terræ.Tć.V.car.modo.IIII.& dim.&.IIII.ać.pti.femp ual.XX.fol De toto.H.sćs eadm.fać & focá.In eadé.V.libi hoes.com.I.car terræ.⁊ LXXX.ać.Tć.V.car.m.II.⁊ .III.ać pti.Tć ual.XXX.fol modo XX.Æcclia LXXX.ać libæ terre.⁊ .I.car.&.I.ać.pti.⁊ ual.V.fol.Totú ht.II.lg in longo.&.VI.qr in lat.⁊ XXII.d &.III.ferding.de geldo*'. Text, Rumble (1986, 401 a, b); translation, Williams and Martin (1992, 1294).

[7] The only other secure reference to an ecclesiastical house in Ixworth is the Priory of St Mary, founded *circa* 1100 by Gilbert Blunt for the Austin canons (Cox, 1907; 1975, 105).

[8] Examples of the reuse of pre-Norman sculpture in architectural contexts are innumerable. Such reuse could be motivated by a sculpture's aesthetic value or simply by the need for building material (cf., Bailey 1980, 45-46).

[9] See note 8.

of a rectangular slab. Its decoration consists of a centrally-placed, wedge-armed cruciform (type B6; ibid.), the shaft of which bisects the slab, terminating against a horizontal bar which likely segmented the slab's decorative programme into two discrete units.[10] A recessed panel of four-cord plaitwork is disposed on either side of the cross-shaft. Like Ixworth 1a, no attempt has been made by the sculptor to emphasize cord-layering at crossing points.

Based on formal and decorative characteristics, these slabs are part of an East Anglian tradition of recumbent and free-standing funerary monuments identified and partially catalogued by Fox (1920-22, 15-45).[11] Recent discoveries attributed to this carving tradition suggest that these monuments were produced in large numbers throughout East Anglia, with particular concentrations in the Cambridge and Peterborough regions (Plunkett 1984, II, 276-278).

The recumbent monuments are rectangular stones, sometimes tapered and occasionally coped with a central ridge, and varying in length from approximately 178 cm (70 in) to 140 cm (55 in) (Fox 1920-22, 20). Coped examples perhaps suggest continuity from the roofed shrines of the seventh to ninth centuries, such as the Hedda Stone at *Medeshamstede* (Peterborough) or the description of St Chad's wooden shrine at Lichfield (HE IV.3, 346-347) and/or the Viking Age hogback memorials of northern England (Walton 1954, 68-77). The free-standing monuments identified by Fox possibly also evoked earlier sepulchral traditions, such as the erection of crosses beside sarcophagi of celebrated ninth-century saints, as at St Alkmund's church in Derby (Radford 1976, pl. IV).

Certain motifs characteristic of the Fenland recumbent slabs' decorative programmes (including cruciforms – both double-headed and those with semicircular shaft-termini) are seemingly expressions of eschatological belief. Double-headed Latin crosses (as depicted on Fenland recumbent slabs Types 1 and 4 and evidenced by Ixworth 1B) are generally interpreted as signs of the Resurrection, possibly evolving from the Gospel accounts that an inscription identifying Christ as 'King of the Jews' ('*Rex Iudaeorum*') was affixed to the True Cross (Matt. 27:37; Mark 15:25; Luke 23:38; John 19:19). Numerous representations of Latin crosses with a second, shorter, transverse bar are extant in various media from the early medieval period.[12] Many are included in Passion cycles, particularly Crucifixion scenes, establishing a cogent relationship between Resurrection and Latin crosses with dual, transverse arms. While the cruciforms' arms on Fenland monuments' Types 1 and 4 are of equal length and are equidistant from either end of the cross-shaft, these subtle digressions from contemporary depictions are probably attributable to the recumbent monuments' rectilinearity – both in general form and through the composition and orientation of their decorative programmes.[13]

Another motif suggestive of eschatological thought is distinctive of Fenland recumbent monuments Types 2 and 5 and is illustrated by Ixworth 1A. Each category exhibits a central cruciform whose shaft terminates in semi-circular motifs.[14] This assemblage is an apparent reference to Golgotha, or Calvary, which the four Gospels record as the site of Christ's crucifixion (Matt. 27:33; Mark 15:22; Luke 23:33; John 19:17). In late classical and early medieval iconography, the True Cross is usually evoked by a cruciform on a hill or a raised base.[15] The existence of such symbolism on the Fenland recumbent monuments is possibly the most compelling evidence that their decorative programmes were inspired by eschatology, particularly the tenet of Resurrection.

Though some of the exemplars from which these recumbent monuments likely derive are associated with monastic contexts, the styles and masterful carving

---

[10] Based on Cambridgeshire evidence, the decoration on the surviving fragment of this slab may have been paralleled on the lost portion (Fox 1920-1922, pls. III-VII).

[11] Grave-covers or coffin-lids decorated with bisecting, wedge-armed cruciforms and interlace panels, small wheel-headed crosses (approximately 61cm in average height), also decorated with interlace, and rectilinear and round-shouldered head- and/or footstones with cruciform decoration, constitute this sculptural group. The recumbent and free-standing monuments are related by similar execution of decorative elements (e.g., three- and four-strand plaitwork and carrick-bends). The recumbent monuments' wedge-armed cruciforms have parallels in Early Christian art (e.g., the lid of the late fourth- or fifth-century sarcophagus of Valerius Amandinus, discovered at Westminster in 1869 (Stanley 1924, 103-109) and in other Anglo-Scandinavian contexts (e.g., the ridged tomb-slab, essentially a hogback, at Hickling, Notts.; Kendrick [1949] 1974, pl. LIII).

[12] Examples include Stadtbibliothek, Trier, Cod. 24, f. 85v (*circa* late tenth century), illustrated in Holländer 1974; 1990, fig. 104; the ivory plaque (*circa* late tenth century) decorating the cover of the *Echternach Gospels* (Germanisches Museum, Nuremberg), illustrated *ibid.*, fig. 126; B.L., Harley 2904, f. 3v (*circa* late tenth century), illustrated in Temple 1976, fig. 142; or B.L., Cotton, Titus D. XXVII, f. 65v (*circa* early eleventh century), illustrated *ibid.*, fig. 246. B.L., Harley 2904, f. 3v, B.L. Cotton, Titus D. XXVII, f. 65v, Stadtbibliothek, Trier, Cod. 24, f. 85v and the *Echternach Gospels* ivory plaque also exhibit a third transverse bar on the True Cross functioning as a foot-rest.

[13] However, a representation of what is probably the True Cross, characterized by symmetry of proportion and equidistance, is preserved in the *Book of Durrow* (Trinity College Library, MS A.4.5 (57), fol. 1v; illustrated in Luce, *et al.* 1960, I, pl. 1v), suggesting that these apparent stylistic choices may also reflect a lengthy Insular iconographic tradition. In contemporary two-dimensional representations of the Crucifixion associated with reformed monasteries either in or near the East Anglian province, the True Cross is depicted with three transverse bars of unequal length (one functioning as Christ's foot-rest). Examples include B.L. Harley 2904, f. 3v (illustrated in Temple 1976, fig. 142; late tenth century; Ramsey Abbey); or B.L. Cotton, Titus, D. XXVII, f. 65v (illustrated *ibid.*, fig. 246; c.1030; New Minster, Winchester).

[14] Type 5 monuments exhibit only one semi-circular shaft-terminus (Fox 1920-22, pl. 5).

[15] Examples include Tatian's *Diatessaron* (c.175 – surviving as a sixteenth-century Persian copy; illustrated in Nordenfalk 1977, 20); English and Irish High Cross of various dates; the Crucifixion scene on the east face of the North Cross at Sandbach, Cheshire (*circa* ninth century; illustrated in Hawkes 2002, 38, fig. 2.5); or Pierpont Morgan Lib. 869, f. 9v (c.990-1000; Canterbury; illustrated in Temple 1976, fig. 171). From the seventh century onwards, Golgotha is sometimes represented by what Hawkes characterizes as an 'amorphous mass of curves' (2002, 41). Examples of such depictions include the seventh- or eighth-century Palestinian casket in the Vatican; the eighth-century frescos at Sta Maria Antiqua (Rome); or the ninth-century Stuttgart Psalter (all illustrated in Schiller 1969; 1971; 1972, II, pls. 329, 328, 355).

associated with such *ateliers* are not represented by this sculptural group. The slabs' limited repertoire of ornamentation and their repetitious, conservative form are suggestive of an industry of funerary masonry (Plunkett 1998, 345). This implies that patrons were not beautifying royal foundations or commemorating saints but were lay or ecclesiastical persons seeking lesser, probably personal, memorials (ibid.). The distribution of these recumbent slabs (together with the related free-standing monuments) is also suggestive of lesser patronage. The sculptures are clustered in the north-west and south-east, somewhat north of the Watling Street, which formed the treaty boundary between Alfred's Wessex and Guthrum's East Anglia in 884. Following the dissolution of monastic hegemonies (such as those centred upon Lichfield and *Medeshamstede*) by the advent of Danish settlement and lordship, new political boundaries arose which seemingly facilitated lay-patronage of masonry (ibid., 346). However, the decoration of the resultant sculptures is not executed in a Scandinavian style nor does it include Scandinavian motifs. This could suggest that particular expressions of lordship were medium-specific and/or dictated by context.

ii) *Stirrup mount*, Suffolk SMR, no. IXW 057-SF21839, *circa* eleventh century (Fig. 3)[16]

Stirrup mount. Used courtesy of the *Portable Antiquities Scheme*

This object is roughly triangular in shape with three almost cylindrical finials projecting from its apex. These finials are arranged at ninety degree intervals around a central fastening hole, and concave borders encircle each finial beneath its terminus. The mount's obverse face is slightly convex, and its triangular section is ornamented by a linear border. On the reverse face, the mount's base projects at an approximately forty-five degree angle. This face is undecorated, though corroded remains of what may have been an iron fitting are visible.[17] The mount's three fastening holes (one centrally-placed at the apex of the triangle and the others parallel in each corner of the base) all contain corroded iron remains (probably rivets).

This is an unusual stirrup mount.[18] Similar mounts have been recovered in Norfolk, Cambridgeshire and Essex. In his typology of stirrup mounts, Williams designates these 'Class A, Type 14'. However, these examples have more elaborate decoration on their triangular portions, and their cylindrical finials terminate in debased zoomorphic heads (Williams 1997, 75-76, fig. 49). This is not evident on the Ixworth example, though it is possible that the zoomorphic decoration has worn away.[19]

iii) *Bridle fitting*, Suffolk SMR, no. IXW 057 SF21839, *circa* eleventh century (Fig. 4)[20]

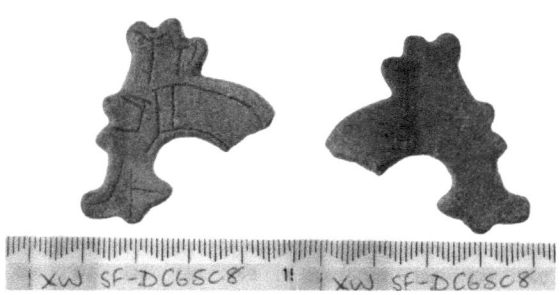

Bridle fitting. Used courtesy of the *Portable Antiquities Scheme*

This object is cast in profile, is slightly bent and is broken at the upward-curving neck. The head (elaborated by a tri-lobed crest) points downwards emphasizing the length of it snout, which terminates in a similar cresting device. The ridge of the creature's snout is also crested, though the protrusions are two in number. The object is further elaborated by two parallel longitudinal grooves on the neck, a combination of two vertical groves surmounted by a zigzag on the head-crest, three longitudinal grooves on the snout-terminus and a rectangular groove which may represent an eye.[21] The creature's form is dragon-like, though it could possibly be a stylized equine. The object's obverse face is undecorated.

This is a fragment of a bridle cheek piece in the form of a Ringerike-style animal head. Similar Ringerike bridle fragments have been recovered from Stoke Holy Cross and Culpho, Suffolk. Based on a complete bridle cheek piece from Angsby, Uppland, Sweden, the Ixworth creature would have adorned one side of the cheek piece

---

[16] http://www.findsdatabase.org.uk/hms/pas_obj.php?type=finds&id=0013EEDD15B013CA
[17] Ibid.

[18] In his consideration of the use of equestrian equipment in late Anglo-Saxon England, Graham-Campbell concurs with Seaby and Woodfield that stirrup mounts were introduced by Scandinavian settlers and that extant examples do not predate the eleventh century (Graham-Campbell 1991, 87-89; and Seaby and Woodfield 1980, 120-122).
[19] http://www.findsdatabase.org.uk/hms/pas_obj.php?type=finds&id=0013EEDD15B013CA
[20] http://www.findsdatabase.org.uk/hms/pas_obj.php?type=finds&id=0013EEDCB5E01955
[21] Ibid.

with a corresponding head on the other side. The bridle would have been secured through a pierced hole at the base of the creatures' necks (Margeson 1997, 34-36, fig. 40).

Conclusion: lordship, stone and metal

Based on Ixworth's extant archaeological record, context seemingly influenced proclamation of social identity. Scandinavian motifs and artistic styles were seemingly independent of ecclesiastical *milieux*. In the Late Saxon period, lay-foundation of a church was a lucrative endeavour. Among other privileges, founders received a portion of all tithes and offerings made to their church (Platt [1981] 1995, 3). If we accept that the patron of the Ixworth grave-slabs was a lord (possibly of mixed Danish/Anglo-Saxon ancestry) or a member of his family and, thus, the likely founder or patron of the manorial church or his descendent, then much of his societal status would be associated with his effective ownership of a church. I have argued elsewhere that the conservative repertoire of motifs and motif-combinations that characterize the decorative programmes of East Anglia's Late Saxon recumbent and free-standing funerary monuments can be interpreted as expressions of eschatological thought, exemplifying the visual culture of East Anglia's tenth- and eleventh-century ecclesiastical system (Reed forthcoming 2009); furthermore, I have posited that display of such motifs in stone proclaimed and reinforced lordly status in ecclesiastical contexts, exhibiting both adherence to the tenets of the Late Saxon Church and prominence in the minster system (Reed 2006 [2007]; Reed forthcoming 2009).[22] Thus, it is reasonable that East Anglian Late Saxon ecclesiastical sculpture is devoid of Scandinavian motifs; such monuments function as memorials and as indicators of elite status within local ecclesiastical and tenurial hierarchies.

Ixworth's extant metal objects proclaim a very different social identity. The equestrian fittings recovered from Ixworth are apparent evidence of a Scandinavian idiom. In secular contexts, Danish identity was seemingly visible and/or asserted. This suggests that Danish culture was vibrant in Late Saxon Suffolk and had not been supplanted by Anglian traditions.[23] Metalwork attributed to the ninth century, stylistically, can be interpreted in the context of colonization as manifestations of cultural dominance. Many of these objects (including 'tortoise' brooches for example) were likely produced in Scandinavia and transported by colonists as valued possessions (Margeson 1997, 6, 10-19). Hybrid objects are probably of later date (*circa* tenth century), illustrating acculturation in northern and eastern England and the apparent advent of an 'Anglo-Scandinavian' identity. 'Janssen Type IIIE Variant' brooches, comprising flat Anglo-Saxon disc forms decorated in the Borre style, are particularly illustrative of this cultural dialogue (Richardson 1993, 21-23). However, those objects decorated in the Ringerike and, perhaps, Urnes styles are firmly associated, chronologically, with Cnut's foundation of a 'Northern Empire' and its apparent promotion of Danish identity. By 1028, Cnut reigned as king in England, Denmark and Norway and had assumed overlordship of Sigtuna, Sweden. Innumerable objects, including the equestrian-fittings from Ixworth, are likely regional manifestations of this Scandinavian empire and its apparent national consciousness.

The vitality of Danish culture in Late Saxon England is also demonstrated by Cnut's court at Winchester and by its surviving literature. While Cnut seemingly pursued a policy of legitimization *vis à vis* the Wessex dynasty through his marriage to Emma of Normandy and by his establishment of a court at Winchester (the former Wessex capital), there was probably a sizable Danish presence in the city in the first quarter of the eleventh century, presumably composed of courtiers and soldiers retained by the king when his invasion fleet returned to Denmark in 1018 (Hooper 1994, 89-100). Some of this retinue was still at the disposal of Cnut's son, Harthacnut, in the 1040s, seemingly confirming their substantial number (ibid., p. 92).

In the 1020s, there is evidence (both material and literary) of cultural syncretism at Winchester. A fragment of a sculpted frieze, perhaps depicting Sigmund – an archetypal character in the origin-myths of both the Danish and English royal houses – was recovered from the Old Minster excavations in 1965 (Biddle 1966, 325, 329-332, pl. 62). The New Minster *Liber Vitae* (BL Stowe 944) records '*Dani*' in confraternity with the minster brethren (Keynes 1996, 104); and Frank has observed considerable English influence in the nine extant skaldic poems composed at Winchester, collectively termed *Knútsdrápur*, suggesting that both English and Old Norse were spoken at Cnut's court (1994, 108-109; Townend 2001, 146). It is probable that Harthacnut's court was equally syncretic, comprised of Anglo-Danish and Anglo-Saxon nobles, Danish housecarls and a multi-lingual dowager-queen.[24]

The *Knútsdrápur* (praise-poetry) has been attributed to Icelandic skalds in the service of Cnut and was recited in the presence of the king and his retainers, probably in official and/or ceremonial contexts (Jesch 2001, 320). Frank has demonstrated that the *Knútsdrápur* evokes many Danish cultural references, suggesting that its

---

[22] Such motifs may also have signalled associations with other churches (e.g., minsters). The Ixworth slabs are akin to another fragmentary example at Bury St Edmunds (Plunkett 1998, 325). Such associations can perhaps be understood in the context of increasing lordly prestige and/or utilizing the influence and power associated with minster foundations. Motif-selection may also have been influenced by sculptors' ethnicity (probably Anglo-Saxon).

[23] Though Scandinavian culture was resilient in Late Saxon East Anglia, other evidence from Ixworth, including a chip-carved, disc-head pin, display the culture's responsiveness to outside stimuli, suggesting that it was continually evolving (see Smith, 1911; 1975, I, 337, fig. 7).

[24] Emma would have been fluent in Flemish, Norman French and English. Having been raised in the Norman court, she may also have been conversant in Old Norse (Stafford 1997, 204).

courtly audience included expatriate Danes. This is illustrated by the frequency with which Cnut is associated with the Danish royal house through use of various devices, including synonyms and kennings. For example, Cnut is identified as '*Skjöldungr*' ('*Scylding*' – an ancient Danish dynastic name) and '*Jóta dróttinn*' ('Lord of the Jutes'; Frank 1994, 110-120). Cnut's conquest of England is portrayed as a tribal battle in which the vanquished are characterized as an 'other': '*ætt drapt, Jóta dróttinn, Játgeirs í för þeiri*' ('Lord of the Jutes, you struck the race of Edgar on that expedition'; text, Jónsson 1912, IB, 232-234; trans., Whitelock 1955, 310-311). Throughout the *Knútsdrápur* (as in skaldic verse and perhaps Scandinavian culture generally), the length, durability and ornamentation of a leader's ships is employed as a metaphor for his martial prowess (Frank 1994, 113-115). Despite Cnut's avowed Christianity, demonstrated by his sponsorship of the Benedictine Reform and by his benefaction of numerous houses, including the New Minster at Winchester, Christianity in the *Knútsdrápur* is portrayed syncretically. In one poem, Óðinn is evoked with '*munka valdr*' ('Lord of the monks' – God; ibid., 119) perhaps suggesting that Denmark's nascent Christianity, introduced by Harald Bluetooth *circa* 965, had not completely displaced pagan traditions. As a conquering force, the Danish retinue at Winchester, some of whom had likely left Denmark in 1015 with Cnut's invasion fleet, may have been only superficially affected by the religion of 'Edgar's race'. It is probable, however, that references to Scandinavian paganism, together with material evidence of Scandinavian culture – specifically metalwork – are suggestive of Cnut's Northern Empire and the promotion of Danish or Scandinavian identity that seemingly accompanied it.

Thus, based on literary evidence of Ixworth's pre-Conquest history, together with its finds' record and supporting evidence (both material and textual) from the royal court at Winchester, it is hypothesized that signification of lordly status in Late Saxon Suffolk was a multivalent process dictated by context. As active participants in the Minster system through foundation and benefaction of manorial churches, lords signified their rank in stone, adopting the preferred medium, styles and iconography of memorialization. As manorial churches also functioned as communities' gathering-places and *de facto* administrative centres, their associated stone monuments also displayed elite status within tenurial hierarchies. Metal objects (whose economic and cultural significance in the early medieval north is often demonstrated by hoards and funerary practice) are seemingly demonstrative of a contemporaneous Scandinavian idiom, supported by historical and literary evidence of Scandinavian colonization and acculturation and by Cnut's foundation of a northern empire in the eleventh century and the contemporaneous promotion of Danish identity at the royal court at Winchester. Therefore, the semiotic systems through which lordship was displayed in Late Saxon Suffolk were apparently both context- and medium-specific, reflecting patrons' adopted or biological ethnicity.

Acknowledgements

I extend sincere thanks to Drs. Zoë Devlin and Caroline Holas-Clark for inviting me to contribute to this project; to Prof. Julian Richards, Dr. Jane Hawkes (York) and Prof. Richard Bailey (Newcastle) who commented on earlier versions of this study; and to Daniel Pett of the *Portable Antiquities Scheme* who assisted with images.

Bibliography

Abels, R. 1988. *Lordship and Military Obligation in Anglo-Saxon England*, California University Press (Berkeley)

Allen, J. and Anderson, J. [1903] 1993. *The Early Christian Monuments of Scotland*, 2 vols., Pinkfoot Press (Balgavies, Angus)

Bailey, R. 1978. 'The chronology of Viking-age sculpture in Northumbria', in J. Lang (ed.), *Anglo-Saxon and Viking Age Sculpture and its Context: Papers from the Collingwood Symposium on Insular Sculpture from 800 to 1066*, B.A.R., British Series, 49 (Oxford): 173-203

Bailey, R. 1980. *Viking Age Sculpture in Northern England*, Collins (London)

Bede. 1969. *Ecclesiastical History of the English People*, B. Colgrave and R. Mynors (eds. and trans.), Clarendon Press (Oxford)

Biddle, M. 1966. 'Excavations at Winchester 1965: Fourth Interim Report', *The Antiquaries Journal*, 46: 308-332

Cameron, K. 1977. 'Scandinavian settlement in the territory of the five boroughs: the place-name evidence. Part II. Place-names in Thorp', in K. Cameron (ed.), *Place-name Evidence for the Anglo-Saxon Invasion and Scandinavian Settlements: Eight studies Collected by Kenneth Cameron*, English Place-Name Society (Nottingham): 139-155

Collingwood, W. [1927] 1989. *Northumbrian Crosses of the Pre-Norman Age*, Llanerch Enterprises (Felinfach, Powys)

Cownie, E. 1998. *Religious Patronage in Anglo-Norman England, 1066-1135*, Boydell (Rochester)

Cox, J. [1907] 1975. 'Religious houses', in W. Page (ed.), *The Victoria History of the Counties of England: Suffolk*, 2 vols., William Dawson & Sons Ltd. (Folkstone, Kent): II, 53-155

Cramp, R. 1982. 'The Viking image', in T. Farrell (ed.), *The Vikings*, Phillimore (London and Chichester): 8-19

Cramp, R. 1984. *Grammar of Anglo-Saxon Ornament*, Oxford University Press (Oxford)

Dodwell, C. 1982. *Anglo-Saxon Art: A New Perspective*, Manchester University Press (Manchester)

Fleming, R. 2001. 'The new wealth, the new rich and the new political style in Late Anglo-Saxon England', *Anglo-Norman Studies*, 23: 12-13

Fox, C. 1920-1922. 'Anglo-Saxon monumental sculpture in the Cambridge district', *Proceedings of the Cambridge Antiquarian Society*, 23: 15-45

Frank, R. 1994. 'King Cnut in the verses of his skalds', in A. Rumble (ed.), *The Reign of Cnut: King of England, Denmark and Norway*, Leicester University Press (London): 106-124

Geake, H. 1992. 'Burial practice in seventh- and eighth-century England', in M. Carver (ed.), *The Age of Sutton Hoo: The Seventh Century in North-Western Europe*, Boydell Press (Woodbridge): 83-94

Graham-Campbell, J. 1991. 'Anglo-Scandinavian equestrian equipment in eleventh-century England', *Anglo-Norman Studies*, 14: 77-89

Hadley, D. 2000. *The Northern Danelaw: its Social Structure, c.800-1100*, Leicester University Press (London & New York)

Härke, H. 2000. 'The circulation of weapons in Anglo-Saxon society', in F. Theuws and J. Nelson (eds.), *Rituals of Power: From Late Antiquity to the Early Middle Ages*, Brill (Leiden and Boston): 377-399

Hawkes, J. 2002. *The Sandbach Crosses: Sign and Significance in Anglo-Saxon sculpture*, Four Courts Press Ltd. (Dublin)

Hawkes, J. 2007. 'Collingwood and Anglo-Saxon sculpture: art history or archaeology?', in R. Moss (ed.), *Making and Meaning in Insular Art: Proceedings of the Fifth International Conference on Insular Art Held at Trinity College Dublin, 25-28 August 2005*, Four Courts Press Ltd. (Dublin): 142-152

Henry, F. [1940] 1965. *Irish Art in the Early Christian Period (to 800 A.D.)*, Methuen (London)

Henry, F. 1964. *Irish High Crosses*, At the Three Candles (Dublin)

Hill, B. [1968] 1984. *English Cistercian Monasteries and their Patrons in the Twelfth Century*, Illinois University Press (Urbana)

Holländer, H. [1974] 1990. *Early Medieval*, trans. C. Hillier, Herbert Press (London)

Hooper, N. 1994. 'Military developments in the reign of Cnut', in A. Rumble (ed.), *The Reign of Cnut: King of England, Denmark and Norway*, Leicester University Press (London): 89-100

Jesch, J. 2001. 'Skaldic Verse in Scandinavian England', in J. Graham-Campbell *et al.* (eds.), *The Vikings and the Danelaw: Select Papers from the Proceedings of the Thirteenth Viking Congress, Nottingham and York, 21-30 August 1997*, Oxbow Books (Oxford): 313-325

Kendrick, T. [1949] 1974. *Late Saxon and Viking Art*, Methuen; Barnes & Noble (London, New York)

Keynes, S. (ed.) 1996. *The Liber Vitae of the New Minster and Hyde Abbey Winchester, British Library Stowe 944, together with leaves from British Library Cotton Vespasian A. VIII and British Library Cotton Titus D. XXVII*, Early English Manuscripts in Facsimile 26, Rosenkilde and Bagger (Copenhagen)

Lang, J. 1973. 'Some late pre-Conquest crosses in Ryedale, Yorkshire: a reappraisal', *Journal of the British Archaeological Association*, series 3, 36: 16-25

Luce, A. *et al.* 1960. *Evangeliorum quattuor Codex Durmachensis. Auctoritate Collegii Sacrosanctae et Individuae Trinitatis Juxta Dublin Totius Codicis Similitudinen Accuratissime Depicti Exprimendam Curavit Typographeum Urs Graf. Prolegomenis Auxerunt Viri Doctissimi Arturus Aston Luce, Georgius Otto Simms, Petrus Meyer, Ludovicus Bieler*, 2 vols., Urs Graf (Olten)

MacGregor, A. and Bolick, E. 1993. *A Summary Catalogue of the Anglo-Saxon Collections (Non-Ferrous Metals), Ashmolean Museum, Oxford*, B.A.R., British Series, 230 (Oxford)

Margeson, S. 1997 *The Vikings in Norfolk*, Norfolk Museums Service (Norwich)

Nash-Williams, V. 1950. *The Early Christian Monuments of Wales*, Wales University Press (Cardiff)

Nenk, B., Margeson, S. and Hurley, M. 1994. 'Medieval Britain and Ireland in 1993', *Medieval Archaeology*, 38: 184-293

Nordenfalk, C. 1977. *Celtic and Anglo-Saxon Painting: Book Illumination in the British Isles, 600-800*, Chatto and Windus (London)

PAS (Portable Antiquities Scheme), find identification no. SF-DCC167, http://www.findsdatabase.org.uk/hms/pas_obj.php?type=finds&id=0013EEDD15B013CA

PAS (Portable Antiquities Scheme), find identification no. SF-DC65C8, http://www.findsdatabase.org.uk/hms/pas_obj.php?type=finds&id=0013EEDCB5E01955

Platt, C. [1981] 1995. *The Parish Churches of Medieval England*, Chancellor Press (London)

Plunkett, S. 1984. *Mercian and West Saxon stone sculpture: schools, styles and patterns of influence*, 2 vols., unpublished Ph.D. dissertation, University of Cambridge

Plunkett, S. 1998. 'Appendix: Anglo-Saxon stone sculpture and architecture in Suffolk', in S. West, *A Corpus of Anglo-Saxon Material from Suffolk*, East Anglian Archaeology Report, 84 (Ipswich)

Radford, C. 1976. 'The church of St Alkmund, Derby', *Journal of the Derbyshire Archaeological and Natural History Society*, 96: 26-61

Reed, M.F. 2006 [2007]. 'Intercultural dialogue in Late Saxon Norwich: the St Vedast Cross', *Quaestio Insularis: Selected Proceedings of the Cambridge Colloquium in Anglo-Saxon, Norse and Celtic*, 7: 119-137

Reed, M.F. (forthcoming, 2009). 'A Late Saxon grave-cover from Thetford, Nf.: form, patronage and production', in M.F. Reed (ed.), *New Voices on Insular Sculpture*, B.A.R., British Series (Oxford)

Reed, M.F. (forthcoming, 2009). *Sculpture and Identity in Late Saxon East Anglia*, Ph.D. dissertation, University of York

Richardson, C. 1993. *The Borre style in the British Isles and Ireland – a reassessment*, unpublished M.Litt. thesis, Newcastle University

Rumble, A. (ed.) 1986. *Domesday Book: Suffolk*, 2 pts., Phillimore (London, Chichester)

Schiller, G. 1969; 1971; 1972. *Iconography of Christian Art*, 2 vols., trans. J. Seligman, Lund Humphries (London)

Seaby, W. and Woodfield, P. 1980. 'Viking stirrups from England and their background', *Medieval Archaeology*, 24: 87-122

Sheehan, M. 1963. *The Will in Medieval England: from the Conversion of the Anglo-Saxons to the End of the Thirteenth Century*, Pontifical Institute of Mediaeval Studies (Toronto)

Smith, R. [1907] 1975. 'Anglo-Saxon remains', in W. Page (ed.), *The Victoria History of the Counties of England: Suffolk*, 2 vols., William Dawson & Sons Ltd. (Folkstone, Kent), I, 325-355

Stafford, P. 1997. *Queen Emma and Queen Edith. Queenship and Women's Power in Eleventh Century England*, Blackwell (Oxford)

Stanley, A. 1924. 'Observations on the Roman sarcophagus lately discovered at Westminster', *Archaeological Journal*, 74: 103-109

Stenton, F. 1943; 1989. *Anglo-Saxon England*, Oxford University Press (Oxford)

Suffolk SMR OS Card, n.d., TL97SW22 (Bury St Edmunds)

Temple, E. 1976. *Anglo-Saxon Manuscripts 900-1066*, Harvey Miller (London)

Tollerton-Hall, L. 2005. *Wills and will-making in Late Anglo-Saxon England*, unpublished Ph.D. dissertation, University of York

Townend, M. 2001. 'Contextualizing the *Knútsdrápur*: skaldic praise-poetry at the court of Cnut', *Anglo-Saxon England*, 30: 145-179

Walton, J. 1954. 'Hogback tombstones and the Anglo-Danish house', *Antiquity*, 28: 68-77

Whitelock, D. 1955. *English Historical Documents, c.500-1042*, Eyre and Spottiswoode (London)

Williams, A. and Martin, G. (eds.) 1992. *Domesday Book: A Complete Translation*, Penguin (London)

Williams, D. 1997. *Late Saxon Stirrup Mounts: a Classification and Catalogue*, Council for British Archaeology, Research Report, 111 (York)

Reassessing remoteness:
Ireland's western off-shore islands in the early medieval period

Sharon A. Greene

Introduction – islands and insularity

The most basic definition of an island as 'a piece of land surrounded by water' does not consider its relationship to anything other than the water that surrounds it. Island archaeology must therefore by necessity engage to some degree with maritime archaeology. However, except perhaps in clear cases of importation of foreign or exotic goods, archaeologists concerned with dry land rarely consider in detail what lies immediately beyond the shoreline. This is perhaps one of the reasons that Ireland's off-shore islands have tended to be studied in isolation. Another is simply their status as islands. Islands' clear physical boundaries mean they have been viewed as conveniently clear units for study by a number of disciplines including geography, local history, archaeology and biogeography. However, while the geographical boundaries of an island are well defined, it is important to remember that island dwellers are not necessarily bound by them (Broodbank 2000, 30).

The literary use of the term 'insular' implies the state of being separate, different or individual and often has the negative connotations of backwardness and narrow-mindedness. It is easy to understand how the basic geographical island inspires the use of such terminology, and there can be little doubt that its use in relation to some island cultures may at times be apt. As well as being considered backwards, islands are also frequently considered special, either in a spiritual way or, particularly in more recent times, in a romantic way. These perceptions have had implicit effects on the study of islands and island cultures.

Modern perceptions of islands naturally influence our interpretations of these landscapes in the past. It is rare to encounter a description of an island that does not include the term 'remote'. This term evokes a somewhat romantic sense of distance and separateness. A visitor to an uninhabited island, particularly one dependant on others for transport to and from it, can be forgiven for feeling cut off, remote or isolated from all they know on the mainland. But can we impose these feelings on an island community for whom that place was home and who perhaps had a strong maritime tradition and suitable boats at their disposal? Surely, a person's perception of remoteness is dependant on where they are standing and their relationship to that place and to the wider world. This suggests that archaeologists studying a past island culture should be very wary of using the adjective remote until certain that it is apt for the population in question.

Perhaps a question we should ask when considering using this term is 'remote from what?'. In the Ireland of today the western Islands are considered physically, economically and even socially distant from the main centres of population and administration in the east of the country, making the use of the term remote apt. However, early medieval Ireland had no central administration or population focus like a capital city from which outlying areas might be considered remote. Thus their remoteness in the early medieval period would have to be based on different foci.

Irish off-shore islands are generally not that far, physically, from the Irish 'mainland'. They usually share the geology of the nearest mainland and/or other islands and are also generally quite small. The vast majority have very poor soil quality and are very exposed to the elements and therefore have limited agricultural potential (though even this has fluctuated over the millennia through human impact). This has meant that their inhabitants have had to exploit the wild resources of sea and coast to a greater or lesser degree over time for survival. Environmentally speaking their subsistence strategies would be very similar to that of the neighbouring 'mainland' coastal dwellers, the only obvious difference really being the mainlanders' potential for less weather-dependant terrestrial travel to more prosperous regions. Whatever the similarities that can be noted between island and mainland communities however, it cannot be denied that both tend to see the island communities as different and distinct. An expression of regional identity from which islands are not immune is the question of costume and an interesting example of this comes from the Inishkea Islands. The most recent inhabitants of the Inishkea islands, off the Belmullet peninsula re-inhabited the islands in the eighteenth century (Dornan 2000, 85). The families came from diverse locations (ibid., 85-88). However, within a generation or two they wore a distinctive costume that marked them out as Inishkea islanders (ibid., 228). We cannot therefore dismiss the impact of islands' separateness on the human imagination and the human experience.

Off-shore island habitation – the nature of the evidence

Until recently, archaeological research on Irish off-shore islands has been almost entirely focussed on the early medieval ecclesiastical remains. Evidence for prehistoric use of islands comes in a number of forms. Apart from the presence of recognised archaeological site types, such as burials, field walls and enclosures, there are occasional artefact discoveries and, perhaps the most enlightening, a growing body of palaeoenvironmental evidence. The former categories attest to activity in the Mesolithic, Neolithic, Bronze Age and Iron Age on various off-shore islands (e.g. Cooney 2004; McCartan 2000; Mitchell 1989, 99-100; Waddell 1994, 82-84). Where palaeoenvironmental investigations have taken place, it has been possible to reconstruct the changing plant ecology and thereby suggest the extent of human impact on the environment over time (Coxon 2001; Mitchell 1989; Molloy et al 2000; Molloy and O'Connell 2004; O'Connell and Ní Ghráinne 1994). This has had interesting results that have challenged some of our preconceptions of island environments. For example, there is evidence for the presence of trees on the Aran Islands into the Later Medieval Period (Molloy and O'Connell 2004, 55) and for the cultivation, albeit small-scale, of cereals on High Island, Co. Galway (Molloy et al 2000, 238 and 240). While the relevant literature suggests that the increase in farming activity that occurs after the 'Late Iron Age Lull' (LIAL), a common feature of west of Ireland pollen cores (Molloy et al 2000, 240) and in Irish pollen cores in general (Weir 1993, 108), is closely associated with the arrival of Christianity (Molloy and O'Connell 2004, 61; Molloy et al 2000, 240), it is interesting to note that it is not always possible to correlate the dated environmental evidence with early ecclesiastical foundations (Hall 2000, 368; O'Connell and Ní Ghráinne 1994, 82). It would, in any case, be dangerous to too closely associate a major shift in agricultural practice with the adoption of a new ideology without corroborative evidence. If we were to accept that this was the case, we would be forced to consider similar possible explanations for similar occurrences in the prehistoric pollen record. The fact that a period of intensive farming on Inis Oírr (400 BC-AD 100; Molloy and O'Connell 2004, 60) overlaps significantly with the LIAL on Inishbofin (179 BC-AD 323; O'Connell and Ní Ghráinne 1994, 81) also raises questions about the nature of the LIAL in general. If, as Weir suggests (1993, 108), it is an indicator of a fall in the overall population of Ireland, the reason for this population decline may have affected the off-shore populations differently.

Since excavation revealed that coastal promontory forts and stone forts had origins as early as the Bronze Age and were not the Iron Age phenomenon they were expected to be (Cotter 1993, 1), the general perception has been that there was little or no activity on the islands in this period. However, the palaeoenvironmental evidence (e.g. Molloy and O'Connell 2004, 54) and some more closely dated excavation evidence (e.g. Mitchell 1989, 100) are suggesting that this is not the case. It is therefore curious that the general assumption about early Christian island foundations is that they were hermitages, a title that implicitly suggests that they were established on empty islands.

Island ecclesiastical foundations were being established from the sixth century AD (with some possible examples as early as the fifth century) as a result of the popular belief among clerics in the Irish church that to leave familiar shores and settle in distant islands was the best way to serve God (Wooding 2001, 84). This self-imposed exile was not necessarily carried out alone; indeed historical examples tend to refer to groups setting out together (e.g. Sharpe 1995, 127; Wooding 2001, 84). Archaeological support for this is seen in the excavation results of the tiny island site of Illaunloughan, Co. Kerry, which lead to its interpretation as a small monastic community, rather than a hermitage (Marshall and Walsh 2005, 125).

While some of these monks may have found uninhabited islands, it is clear others did not, for example the Irish clerics who arrived on the inhabited Isle of Wight, off the south coast of England, in AD 891 (Wooding 2001, 84). Even if they began as isolated hermitages, they did not necessarily remain so for long. There is evidence to suggest that pilgrimage to some of the island sites began in the early centuries of Christianity (Herity 1989, 123). The construction of a sophisticated watermill on High Island suggests that its community was part of a network through which such technical innovations had travelled across Europe (Rynne 2000, 198). It is not the aim of this paper to argue for or against the existence of insular hermitages, rather to question the general use of the term 'remote' in relation to these sites by questioning the remoteness of these islands in the early medieval mind, in as far as is possible through the use of contemporary texts.

Islands in early medieval texts

While there is little direct discussion of the western Irish islands in early medieval religious texts, we can still make observations about how they were perceived by early medieval clerics. We know, for example, that Britain and Ireland were considered to be situated on the edge of the civilised world (O'Loughlin 1997, 14). The islands were thus literally the last fragments of land on the edge of the vast Ocean that encircled the known terrestrial world. The tradition of *peregrinatio*, the self-imposed exile described above, may mean that the island monks of Britain and Ireland envisaged themselves as being in a remote position battling demons in the Ocean (O'Loughlin 1997, 15). Tales of sea monsters being subdued and storms being calmed in the saints' *Lives* are symbolic of the fight between good and evil (ibid., 22; e.g. Sharpe 1995, 197-8). In the context of the church, these places were remote both from the head of the church in Rome and also from the perceived centre of the world in Jerusalem (O'Loughlin 1996, 110).

However, early Irish writers, unlike their Mediterranean fathers, frequently used water imagery in a positive sense. Compared to the writers of the Bible for whom it was a distant and dangerous thing, the Ocean was much closer to the island monks of the Atlantic coastline and they would have appreciated not only its real dangers but also its benefits. We know from the *Lives* that they had excellent knowledge of winds, tides and the dangers of seafaring (O'Loughlin 1997, 20) and they carried out

Fig. 1. Islands in Clew Bay viewed from the north shore at Rossturk.

Fig. 2. Inishderry in Broadhaven Bay, north-west Co Mayo.

numerous sea journeys for a variety of reasons (Sharpe 1995, 23 and 73). About AD 825, an Irish monk named Dicuil, based in the Carolingian court, wrote about the various islands that existed off the Irish and British coasts claiming, '[i]n some of these I have dwelt, some I have entered, some I have only seen, some I have read about' (Howlett 1999, 129), suggesting he was well travelled. Moreover he wrote about information he got from another priest who had visited the Faroe Islands where he encountered Irish monks (ibid., 130). There is also evidence of Irish clerics having made it as far as Iceland (Vésteinsson 2000, 164-5).

Even without direct archaeological evidence for seafaring boats from this period, this information suggests a sophisticated level of seafaring and the language used to describe boats makes reference to a few different types both of wooden and skin construction (Wooding 2001, 80). It is not clear to what degree the islands themselves were considered special in a monastic context, though they certainly had some symbolic function in tales such as St Brendan's *Voyage* (O'Meara 1991). The last 'real' island encountered in this allegorical tale, the 'Island of Delights', was an island where the perfect monastic life was led, suggesting that such a life brought one close to heaven (or in this case the 'Island of the Promised Land') (O'Loughlin 1999, 17). Whatever the function of islands in religious texts, it is clear that most of the real island foundations were within the sphere of travel and influence of others, not the solitary dwellings implied in most descriptions of hermitages. This suggests that even those considered distant were not necessarily permanently isolated or remote. Sharpe has noted that any isolation suffered by the Iona community was generally the result of periods of bad weather when it was too dangerous to travel, rather than of any 'supposed remoteness' (1995, 23). He also notes that Adomnán, Columba's biographer and abbot of Iona in the late seventh century, gives the impression that these periods were temporary inconveniences and that the sea was 'much more an aid to communication than an obstacle' (ibid.). Secular texts do not deal in detail with seafaring, however observations on the seafaring associated with monastic communities like Iona must reflect the general picture of sea travel and trade to some degree.

As mentioned above, there tends to be a perception of the shoreline as a boundary, however it is clear from the early medieval law tracts that territory could be extended beyond it. According to Early Irish law, anything washed up on shore was the property of the adjacent landowner and anything found floating in the sea beyond the distance of 'nine waves' was the property of the finder (Kelly 1988, 108). That implies that anything floating inshore of that distance was also within the property of the adjacent landowner. Unfortunately how far the distance of 'nine waves' was is unknown. It seems probable that at least some islands were within this distance and therefore feasibly part of the relevant mainland territory, for example some of the Clew Bay islands or Inishderry in North Mayo (Figs. 1 and 2). This was not necessarily the case and the sea, no matter how wide or narrow the crossing, could have formed a boundary in the same way that rivers and other natural phenomena did.

Secular tales rarely mention islands, but a notable exception is *Táin Bo Flidhais*, a pre-tale to the more famous *Táin Bo Cuailnge*, which mentions a number of Co. Mayo's off-shore islands. Surviving versions of the tale belong to the twelfth and later centuries AD, however the tale is set in the first century AD (Aldridge 1961, 117-8). The story follows the progress of a number of characters through the territory of Connacht, but of

Table 1:

No. on map	Name(s) in text	Location
25	Dun inbir da tonn	Dooniver, Achill Island
26	'cave of Acaill'	Unknown location on Achill
27	Acaill	Unknown location on Achill
28	Inis caéin Iarthir	Inishkea South
29	Inis caéin Airthir	Inishkea North
30	Oilén muighi mín	Annagh Island
31	Inis na Sgáil	Duvillaun Mor
32	Inis Finnáin	Unknown

Table 1: Suggested identification of island placenames on Engán's Route in Táin Bó Flidhais (after Aldridge 1962, with alterations).

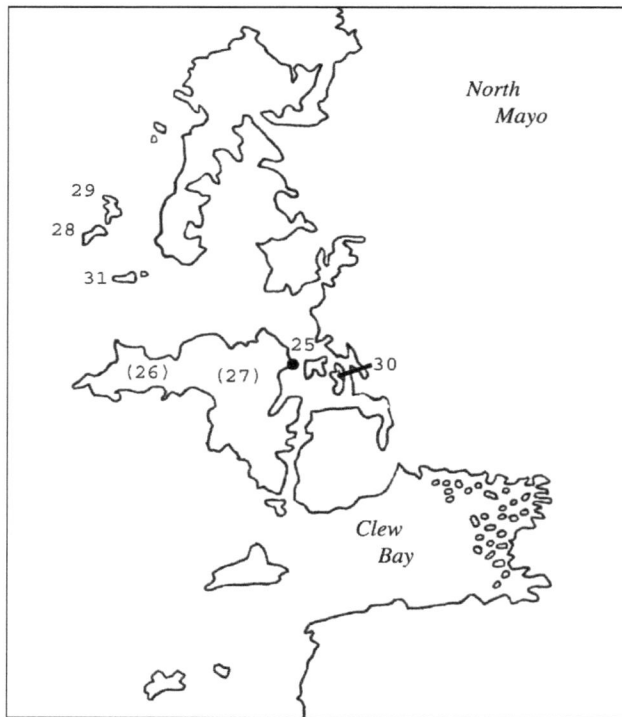

Fig. 3: identification of island sites on Engán's Route in Táin Bó Flidhais (see table 1).

Fig. 4. Low lying Annagh Island viewed from the east shore of Inishbiggle with the Mayo mountains in the background.

Fig. 5. Duvillaun Mór viewed from Inishkea North with Achill Island behind it.

particular interest is the route taken by one of Aillil's two messengers, Engán, sent to call a mustering of the chiefs of the Gamanraid (Aldridge 1961, 219). This tribe appear as one of the less influential, but nonetheless respected tribes in the province of Connacht in later centuries AD (Breathnach 2003, 34), however it has been argued on linguistic grounds that they are the 'Magnantae' who feature on Ptolemy's map in this region (Mac an Bhaird 1993, 7). This suggests they were prominent in the second century AD, fitting in relatively closely with the chronological setting of the *Táin Bó Flidhais* and their retained respect in later centuries.

The route taken by Engán included eight island sites, each associated with a different person or band, on six islands (table 1; Fig. 3). Achill appears three times, but only one of the three locations can be identified with any certainty. This is *Dun Inbir Da Tonn*, 'fort of the bay of two waves', which is identified with Dooniver on the north-west corner of Achill Island, overlooking the sound between Achill and Inishbiggle through which runs a fast tidal stream (Aldridge 1962, 27). Of the remaining two sites, one is called 'the cave of Achill', but the location of neither is known. *Inis Caein Iarthir* and *Inis Caein Airthir*, translated as the western and eastern 'fair isle' are identified as Inishkea North and South (ibid., 28). The Tithe Applotment Book, compiled in 1832, refers to 'Innishkea East' and 'Innishkea West' (Dornan 2000, 86 and 88) and even today, the descendants of the last Inishkea islanders refer to the settlements on these islands as West Town (South Island) and East Town (North Island) (ibid., 50).

Oilen Muighi Min translates as the 'island of the smooth plain' (Aldridge 1962, 28). Aldridge contradicts himself in his identification of this island by firstly suggesting that the description matches Annagh Island, between Inishbiggle and the mainland at Ballycroy and then changing this to the Annagh Peninsula in the north of the Mullet, near Inishglora which is 'almost an island' and further adds that 'none of the islands off the coast could possibly fit the description of smooth plain' (Aldridge 1962, 28). He was however probably correct in his first identification of Annagh Island, which is indeed a low 'smooth' island, in contrast to the neighbouring mainland and the undulating Inishbiggle (Fig. 4). Aldridge suggests that either *Inis na Sgail* /'shadow isle' or *Inis Finnain* could be either Duvillaun Mór or Inishglora (1962, 28). The identification of *Inis na Sgail* as Duvillaun Mór is supported by the form it takes when viewed from the Inishkea Islands, where it looks like a shadow at the base of the mountains of Achill (Fig. 5). This leaves *Inis Finnain* as unidentified. Engán is also sent to Angus, son of Echtach of Ára (Aran Islands, Co. Galway) (Aldridge 1962, 22). The presence of Aran on the itinerary is obviously problematic as it lies a long distance from all other sites in the tale.

The significance of this information from *Táin Bo Flidhais* is twofold. Firstly it suggests secular settlement on the islands and secondly, it suggests that the territory of the Gamanraidh extended beyond the mainland, i.e. the islands were elements of a larger political entity and their presence across the sea did not exclude them. The islands are thus portrayed as *túatha*, in much the same way that they are more recently considered townlands.

Conclusion

Ireland's off-shore islands have not seen continuous occupation from their initial colonisation to recent times. Their human populations have waxed and waned to varying degrees over the millennia. The ecclesiastical nature of the majority of the historical evidence from the early medieval period has given the impression that the religious foundations on the islands were established by clerics setting out to find 'a place of retreat in the ocean' (Sharpe 1995, 127 and 196), a term that implies isolation, and the high visibility of the resulting church and monastic sites in comparison to remains of other periods and activities has been seen, in the past, to support this (Greene 2008). The tendency has been therefore to describe these sites as hermitages, even where evidence exists for their growth into larger establishments (e.g. Rynne 2000, 206).

It is proposed here that the term 'remote' is not a helpful one in the context of island archaeology. It should not be abandoned completely as it is a valid descriptive term, however great care should be taken before applying it. As always in archaeological interpretation, the adjective should be seen to fit the evidence rather than *vice versa*. Apart from the physical position of the island, among the factors to be taken into account are some of those fundamental to the study of island cultures, i.e. resources and subsistence strategies, material culture (including evidence of imported goods), modes of transport. The apparent convenience of island boundaries to research is artificial and, unless complete self-sufficiency and isolation can be proven, the broader seascape and islandscape must be taken into account.

Activity on the sea leaves no marks on the surface but island habitation, perhaps more than general coastal habitation, serves as reminder of this activity and highlights the connectivity of the sea and the potential extent to which it was used. Thus island archaeology can have an important role in bridging the gap between terrestrial and maritime archaeology and indeed in highlighting the artificiality of the perceived gap between sea and land.

Acknowledgements

My PhD research is funded by an Irish Research Council for the Humanities and Social Sciences Government of Ireland Postgraduate Scholarship.

Bibliography

Aldridge, R.B. 1961. 'The routes described in the story called Táin Bó Flidhais', *Journal of the Royal Society of Antiquaries of Ireland*, 91: 117-127; 219-228

Aldridge, R.B. 1962. 'The routes described in the story called Táin Bó Flidhais', *Journal of the Royal Society of Antiquaries of Ireland*, 92: 21-40

Bhreathnach, E. 2003. 'Tales of Connacht: *Cath Airtig, Táin Bo Flidhais, Cath Leitreach Ruibhe*, and *Cath Cumair*', *Cambrian Medieval Celtic Studies*, 45: 21-42

Broodbank, C. 2000. *An Island Archaeology of the Early Cyclades*, Cambridge University Press (Cambridge)

Cooney, G. 2004. 'Neolithic worlds; islands in the Irish Sea', in V. Cummings and C. Fowler (eds.), *The Neolithic in the Irish Sea. Materiality and Traditions of Practice*, Oxbow Books (Oxford): 145-159

Cotter, C. 1993. 'Western Stone Fort Project: interim report', *Discovery Programme Report*, 1 Royal Irish Academy/Discovery Programme (Dublin): 1-19

Coxon, P. 2001. 'The quaternary history of Clare Island', in J.R. Graham (ed.), *New Survey of Clare Island Volume 2: Geology*, Royal Irish Academy (Dublin) 87-112

Dornan, B. 2000. *Mayo's Lost Islands: The Inishkeas*. Four Courts Press (Dublin)

Greene, S.A. 2008. "The isles afar off' – taking a new look at Ireland's holy islands', in J. Connolly and M. Campbell (eds.), *Comparative Island Archaeologies*, B.A.R., International Series, 1829 (Oxford): 233-246

Hall, V.A. 2000. 'Pollen analytical investigations of the Irish landscape, AD500-1650', *Peritia – Journal of the Medieval Academy of Ireland*, 14: 342-71

Herity, M. 1989. 'The antiquity of *An Turas* (the pilgrimage round) in Ireland', reprinted in M. Herity (ed.), 1995 *Studies in the Layout, Buildings and Art in Stone of Early Irish Monasteries*, The Pindar Press (London): 91-143

Howlett, D. 1999. 'Dicuill on the islands of the north' *Peritia – Journal of the Medieval Academy of Ireland*, 13: 127-34

Kelly, F. 1988. *A Guide to Early Irish Law*, Early Irish Law Series iii. Dublin Institute of Advanced Studies (Dublin)

Mac an Bhaird, A. 1993. 'Ptolemy revisited', *Ainm – Bulletin of the Ulster Place-Name Society*, 5: 1-20

Marshall, J.W. and Walsh, C. 2005. *Illaunloughan Island, An Early Medieval Monastery in County Kerry*, Wordwell, (Bray)

McCartan, S.B. 2000. 'The utilization of island environments in the Irish Mesolithic: agendas for Rathlin Island', in A. Desmond, G. Johnson, M. McCarthy, J. Sheehan and E. Shee-Twohig (eds.), *New Agendas in Irish Prehistory: Papers in Commemoration of Liz Anderson*, Wordwell (Bray): 15-30

Mitchell, F. 1989. *Man and Environment in Valencia Island*, Royal Irish Academy (Dublin)

Molloy, K. and O'Connell, M. 2004. 'Holocene vegetation and land-use dynamics in the karstic environment of Inis Oírr, Aran Islands, western Ireland: pollen analytical evidence evaluated in light of the archaeological record', *Quaternary International*, 113: 41-64

Molloy, K., Fuller, J.L. and Conaghan, J. 2000. 'Vegetation and land-use history on High Island: the results of preliminary investigations', in J.W. Marshall and G.D. Rourke (eds.), *High Island, An Irish Monastery in the Atlantic*, Town House (Dublin): 233-243

O'Connell, M. and Ní Ghráinne, E. 1994. 'Palaeoecology', in P. Coxon and M. O'Connell (eds.), *Clare Island and Inishbofin*, Field Guide no.7, Irish Quaternary Association (IQUA): 61-101

O'Loughlin, T. 1996. 'The view from Iona: Adomnán's mental maps', *Peritia* 10: 98-122

O'Loughlin, T. 1997. 'Living in the Ocean', in C. Bourke (ed.), *Studies in the Cult of Saint Columba*, Four Courts Press (Dublin): 11-23

O'Loughlin, T. 1999. 'Distant Islands: The topography of holiness in the *Nauigatio Santi Brendani*', in M. Glasscoe (ed.), *The Medieval Mystical Tradition – England, Ireland and Wales*, Woodbridge (Suffolk): 1-20

O'Meara, J.J. (trans) 1991. *The Voyage of Saint Brendan "Journey to the Promised Land"*, Colin Smythe Ltd (Buckinghamshire)

Rynne, C. 2000. 'The early medieval monastic watermill', in J.W. Marshall and G.D. Rourke (eds.), *High Island, An Irish monastery in the Atlantic*, Town House (Dublin), 185-214

Sharpe, R. (trans.) 1995. *Adomnán of Iona: Life of St Columba*, Penguin Classics (London)

Vésteinsson, O. 2000. 'The archaeology of *Landnám*: early settlement in Iceland', in W.W. Fitzhugh and E.I. Ward, (eds.), *Vikings – the North Atlantic Saga*, Smithsonian Institution Press (Washington) & National Museum of Natural History (London): 164-174

Waddell, J. 1994. 'The archaeology of the Aran Islands', in J.Waddell, J.W. O'Connell and A. Corff (eds.), *The Book of Aran*, Tír Eolas Press (Kinvara), 75-105

Weir, D. 1993. 'A palynological study in County Louth. Interim Report', *Discovery Programme Reports*, 1: 104-109

Wooding, J.M. 2001. 'St Brendan's Boat: dead hides and the living sea in Columban and related hagiography', in J.Carey, M. Herbert and P.Ó Riain (eds.), *Studies in Irish Hagiography*, Four Courts Press (Dublin),77-92

Romans go home? An archaeological and historical exploration of the cult of saints in late antique Britain

Michael Garcia

This paper will discuss research currently underway for a PhD researching saints' cults in Britain *c.*300-700; it aims to explore the evidence for cults other than St Alban's via several approaches: historical, archaeological and interdisciplinary. I shall present the evidence offered by textual sources, followed by archaeological evidence which might corroborate these sources, then discuss an archaeologically determined approach, and finally an interdisciplinary approach to reconcile these methods.

Scholars studying Late Antique Britain must confront the paucity of documents. Due to the sparse textual evidence and dependence on later historical sources such as Bede, the dominant view until the 1980s was that the fabric of Romano-British society gradually dissolved, leaving no trace of political or economic institutions after the mid-fifth century. Christianity was abandoned in the east and then reintroduced by Irish missionaries and the mission of St Augustine to Kent. In this view, the Saxons dominated late fifth-century Britain, while the Britons reverted to an Iron Age lifestyle, and were eventually conquered by the Saxons in the late sixth century.

Questioning of this view, and some of the inherited definitions on which it rests, began in earnest about twenty years ago. Since then understanding has been continually revised, with acknowledgment that earlier perceptions were oversimplified. A more complex picture is emerging. Many scholars, such as Simon Esmonde Cleary (2001), Ken Dark (2000), Mark Handley (2001) and Richard Sharpe (2002), have begun to apply the term 'Late Antiquity' to Britain, which had previously been applied exclusively to mainland Europe.

For the purposes of this piece, the phrase 'Late Antiquity' is used with the definition set out by Simon Esmonde Cleary (2001) in his article 'The Roman to Medieval Transition': the period beginning with the fourth century AD and lasting at least until the seventh century, covering the territory of the Roman Empire. The phrase is used in hopes of establishing an integrative framework for discourse that can incorporate disparate material, and reintegrating Britain into the context of the continent. While this perpetuates problems of periodisation, I find it the most useful way to describe the chronological range of my research.

Textual evidence

Writers in Late Antiquity believed that Christianity was introduced to Britain during the Roman period and that it survived after the disintegration of Roman administration. The cult of St Alban may be the only one which had its origins in the Roman period and continued into the later Middle Ages, but it was probably not the only saint's cult that developed in Roman Britain. The primary sources for late antique Britain are scarce and have long been known. They do, however, mention the existence of cults other than Saint Alban's. The surviving Christian communities may or may not have been scattered, but the cult of saints was an important part of Christian tradition.

Passing references by Tertullian, Origen, Athanasius and Sulpicius Severus indicate that Christianity reached Britain by the third century, and that British bishops attended important synods throughout the fourth century. Aside from these texts, primary sources that witness Christianity in Late Antique Britain include Victricius of Rouen's *De Laude Sanctorum*, the anonymous *Passio Albani*, Constantius of Lyon's *Vita Sancti Germani*, Gildas' *De Excidio Britonum*, and the correspondence between Gregory the Great and St Augustine of Canterbury, aka the *Libellus Responsionum*. These sources all refer to martyr saints.

Victricius of Rouen's sermon, *De Laude Sanctorum*, written around AD 396, was produced for the occasion of the arrival of relics sent to Rouen from Ambrose of Milan (Clark 1999; 2001).[1] Victricius employed a language and format traditionally reserved for imperial panegyrics, which suggests that Victricius equated the relics the same status as a visiting emperor (Clark 1999). Victricius' sermon was intended to convince his audience of the legitimacy of the translation of saints' relics, something with which a late antique audience may not have been entirely comfortable, considering the strict Roman laws proscribing burial of the dead to extra-mural areas. This sermon underlines the tension between the emerging cult of relics and Roman notions about the place of the dead (Clark 2001).

Victricius' sermon also provides evidence for the situation in Britain. At the beginning of his sermon, it is mentioned that he has just returned from Britain, having travelled there to make peace at the request of British priests and bishops. The sermon is frustratingly vague about the details of his trip, but the leading interpretation is that he went there to quell a heresy, as did Germanus of Auxerre in AD 429. If this is the case, the heresy in question could not have been Pelagianism, because it was not declared heretical until after the *De Laude Sanctorum* was written. Victricius stated that his visit to Britain concerned saints' relics, although he provides no specifics and mentions no saints' names. At the end of the sermon, he describes several saints, including one who parted the waters in his haste to martyrdom. This is

---

[1] The sermon is the only extant material by Victricius. Clarke believes its survival is likely due to it being falsely attributed to Ambrose.

thought to be St. Alban, because it echoes events described in the *Passio Albani*. The text of the sermon reads '…ille inter manus carnificum, ne qua mora fieret properanti, iussit redire fluminibus' (Victricius 1985).[2] Demeulenaere makes the comparison to the *Passio Albani* (Meyer 1904; Victricius 1985). This is an appealing hypothesis, given that the sermon was composed shortly after Victricius returned from Britain, where he might have heard the story of this martyr. However, because Victricius did not name the saint who parted the waters, and the earliest version of the *Passio Albani* has been dated to the mid-fifth century (Sharpe 2001), we cannot say with any certainty that it is a reference to Alban.

The anonymous *Passio Albani* relates Alban's martyrdom. An anonymous Christian fleeing persecution was given refuge by Alban. Alban took his place when the authorities came to Alban's residence looking for the Christian. Alban was tried, convicted, and sentenced to execution. As he was led to the site of the execution, he parted the waters of a river because the bridge was too crowded to walk across. This so impressed Alban's intended executioner that he converted to Christianity on the spot and rather than execute Alban he joined him in martyrdom. When Alban reached the site of his execution on top of a hill outside town, he performed another miracle by calling up a well of water because he was thirsty. As Alban was beheaded, the new executioner's eyes popped out of his skull.

The *Passio* also states that Germanus of Auxerre visited the tomb of Alban and exchanged relics, taking some from Alban's grave and leaving some from the portable reliquary he carried around his neck.

There are three extant versions of the text, labelled T, E and P, which stand for Turin, Excerpt, and Paris, respectively. Wilhelm Meyer published all three in 1904 (Meyer 1904).[3] The *Passio Albani* does not specify a location for the martyrdom, but the topography described broadly accords with Verulamium (Biddle 1986).[4] Meyer postulated that the transmission history of these variant texts is as follows. The oldest manuscript, containing text T and produced at Nôtre Dame de Soissons in the late eighth century, represents the oldest version of the text, written in the early sixth century. This was then abridged to form text E (for 'excerpt'), which was then redacted to form text P, found in a manuscript written around the beginning of the tenth century at Saint Maur-les-Fossés.

Richard Sharpe has argued that Meyer misinterpreted the sequence of composition for T, E and P (Sharpe 2001). Sharpe presented an alternative interpretation in which text E is the parent text of both T and P, observing that the entire text of E is found in both T and P, while the discrepancies between E and T are not found in P, and likewise the discrepancies between P and E are not find in T. Sharpe went on to posit that text E represents an account of Alban's martyrdom that was originally displayed on placards at the site of the basilica dedicated to Alban in Auxerre founded by Germanus after his visit to the shrine of Alban in 429, and was composed in Germanus' lifetime, predating the composition of the *Vita Sancti Germani* by Constantius of Lyon. In consequence, Sharpe stated that no certain date can be assigned to the martyrdom of Alban, since text E provides no clue to the date except for the phrase *tempore persecutionis*, 'in the times of persecution'. If Sharpe is correct about the text predating the *Vita Sancti Germani*, then the *Passio Albani* is the earliest surviving reference to Alban by name, or indeed any named British saint.

The *Vita Sancti Germani*, written around AD 470, includes several passages that relate Germanus' two trips to Britain to fight the Pelagian heresy (Constantius 1920; Noble and Head 1995). After defeating the Pelagian heretics in a contest of miracles, Germanus petitioned Alban to give thanks to God.

> Conpressa itaque perversitate damnabili eiusque auctoribus confutatis animisque omnium fidei puritate conpositis, sacerdotes beatum Albanum martyrem, acturi Deo per ipsum gratias, petierunt (Constantius 1920, 262).[5]

This is the only mention of a British cult in the *Vita Germani*. His first visit to Britain is also attested in Prosper of Aquitaine's *Chronica*.

Gildas' *De Excidio Britonum*, composed sometime around or after the year 500, is the only surviving source from an author who was living and writing in late antique Britain. Thomas O'Sullivan (1978) has presented a cogent argument that *De Excidio Britonum* was written sometime between 515-530 AD, and puts to rest any doubt as to the authenticity of Gildas' authorship. Ian Wood (1984) has suggested a date of composition between AD 485 and AD 530.

Whilst *De Excidio Britonum* was not intended as a historical tract, it provides significant historical data. Gildas claimed that in Britain there were many shrines to martyrs, some of which are cut off by the *lugubri divortio barbarorum*, the grievous barbarian partition (*DEB*, ch. 10, p. 92). The meaning of this phrase is unclear. It could be interpreted that the Saxons had already claimed the areas of these shrines or only that Saxon controlled

---

[2] '…this one, in the hands of the executioners, told the rivers to draw back, lest he should be delayed in his haste.' Translation from Clark (1999).

[3] T is represented by manuscript Turin, Biblioteca Nazionale, MS D. V. 3; E (excerpt) is represented by four manuscripts: London, BL MS Add. 11880 (s.ix); Autun, Seminaire, MS 34 (s. ix/x); London, Gray's Inn, MS 3 (s. xii); Einsiedeln, Stiftsbibliothek MS 248 (s. xii); and P by Paris, Bibliotheque Nationale de France, MS lat. 11748.

[4] The description could also apply to many other contemporary settlements. However, the text refers to an arena outside of the walls of the city, which is absent at Verulamium. The description is actually more likely to be a rhetorical device, a *locus amoenus* description, and not intended to be literal.

[5] 'And so, this damnable heresy being crushed and its authors confuted and the souls of all the faithful restored to the true faith, the priests petitioned the blessed martyr Alban to give thanks to God.'

territory was between Gildas and these shrines, or something else entirely. He provided the names of only three martyrs: Alban of Verulamium and Julius and Aaron of Caerleon. There is a brief description of Alban's martyrdom, possibly based on the *Passio* text E (Sharpe 2001). It should be noted that while Gildas mentioned that Alban was a citizen of Verulamium, he did not explicitly state that this is where he was martyred.

Although they do not reveal the specific details we might want from them, these primary sources convey important points about Christianity in Late Antique Britain. Victricius and Constantius' portrayal of Britain contrasts with that of Gildas and Bede and also of some modern historians, including William Frend, whose work has repeatedly argued that Christianity was all but gone from Britain by the mid fifth century, with no direct line of continuity between the Romano-British and Anglo-Saxon church (Frend 1968; 1974; 1979; 1982; 1984; 1992; 1996; 2002; 2004). In the *Vita Sancti Germani*, Constantius did not claim that the Saxons had political or cultural dominance on the island. In fact, Germanus is shown leading the British in a decisive victory over the Saxons during his first visit. Regardless of the veracity of this episode, Constantius must have considered it believable for his late fifth-century audience. It is not explicitly stated, but it is implied that the British population is for the most part Christian. Britain is not portrayed as undergoing any cataclysmic decline, nor is it described as isolated from the other provinces of the Roman Empire, except perhaps in the lack of a charismatic bishop like Germanus. Neither do these sources depict the British reverting to paganism. Although Gildas described cities being abandoned, this is not unique. When Constantius visited Clermont in 473 he found the city deserted, due to civil strife as much as barbarian invasion. This echoes Gildas' description of the situation in Britain during the Anglo-Saxon migration, demonstrating that Britain should not necessarily be viewed as an exceptional case as far as the outcome of barbarian invasions (Sims-Williams 1983).

In the correspondence between Gregory the Great and Augustine of Canterbury, the *Libellus Responsionum*, there is a very brief but curious mention of a saint's cult encountered by Augustine after he settles in Kent (Deanesly and Grosjeans 1959). Apparently, Augustine encountered some native British venerating Saint Sixtus, who is described as a martyr. However, devotees of the cult had forgotten all the tradition and history of the cult except for the name of the saint himself. Augustine wrote to Gregory asking how he should handle the situation. Gregory, fearing these Christians to be worshipping false relics, sent to Augustine relics of Saint Sixtus, a former Pope who had been martyred, to replace whatever the Britons had hitherto been venerating. Gregory was not confident that the British could have been worshipping an authentic martyr who happened to be named Sixtus, a common Roman name.

Rob Meens (1994; 1996) and Ian Wood (1995; 2000b) have argued that the questions posed by Augustine to Gregory found in the *Libellus Responsionum* indicate that British clergy evangelised the English before the arrival of Augustine. Questions concerning ritual purity in relation to entering a church are unlikely to have been raised by pagans. Rather, they indicate the influence of British clergy, as similar questions emerge in later correspondence between insular churchmen. Wood argued that these questions indicate Augustine's contact with British clergy was more extensive than Bede suggests (Wood 2000b).

The history of British Christianity was deliberately suppressed by Anglo-Saxon writers, especially Bede. He emphasised the primacy of Rome and the Augustinian mission while neglecting the influence of the native British church as well as the church in Gaul (Wood 1994). In the *Historia Ecclesiastica*, Bede establishes the British as the villains of the narrative even as he writes them out of history (Wood 2000a). However, upon examination, glimpses of British Christianity are revealed.

Bede recounted Alban's martydom (*HE* I.7). Bede is the first extant source to link Verulamium with the site of his execution. He also stated that a church was built at Verulamium and that miracles happened there up to his day, implying the continuous presence of a Christian community at the site. If this is the case, then the community must have been British Christians up until, and probably after, Augustine's mission of AD 597.

His account of Alban's martyrdom closely matches that of the Paris manuscript for Alban's passion. Julius and Aaron are mentioned as well, but as in Gildas, no information is provided other than their name and that they were from Caerleon.

Bede also related an encounter between Augustine and a group of British bishops at a site that would later be called Augustine's Oak (*HE* II.2). Augustine encouraged the bishops to help him in his mission to convert the English. The British bishops asked for time to deliberate and call for a second conference, to be held at the aforesaid oak. Augustine agreed, and then the bishops asked the advice of a hermit. The hermit advised them to test Augustine's humility by letting him arrive at their meeting place first and then observe if he rose to greet them. When Augustine did not do so, the British bishops refused to help him. Augustine was offended and prophesied bad tidings for the British. His prophecy was later fulfilled when many British monks from Bangor were killed in a battle. Bede's description of the slaughter as divine retribution is an indication of his antipathy towards the British clergy. Clare Stancliffe (1999) has deconstructed this particular episode, arguing that Bede may have used a British source for his information, pointing out that the British appear to act reasonably, and that the narrative portrays events that occur away from Augustine.

Bede's antipathy towards the British is apparent in other passages of the *Historia Ecclesiastica*. Bede reported that

Chad was consecrated by Wine, bishop of West Saxons, along with two British bishops (*HE* III.28). Afterwards, Chad was informed by Theodore that his consecration was not regular because of the two British Bishops, and he therefore needed to be re-consecrated in the Catholic manner (*HE* IV.2).

Stephanus provided a more detailed description of Chad's consecration in his *Vita Wilfridi*. Stephanus explained that Chad's original consecration was irregular because the two British Bishops were Quartodecimans, meaning they celebrated Easter between the fourteenth and twenty-first day after the full moon, rather than between the fifteenth and twenty-second, as was the custom of Rome.

Perhaps the best evidence for deliberate suppression of British Christianity is St Ninian and Whithorn. There is very little we can say with certainty about Ninian. It is commonly believed that he was a fifth-century bishop based at Whithorn, who evangelised the Picts. However, Thomas Owen Clancy (2001) has presented a radical new interpretation arguing that the name Ninian is a result of a scribal error mistaking *Uinniau* for *Ninniau*, and that *Uinnia* was in fact St. Finnian of Moville, a correspondent of Gildas, securing his floruit to the sixth century. This would place Ninian in the sixth century, making a strong case for a thriving British church in Late Antiquity. However, MacQueen (2005) has rebutted Clancy's claims on the grounds that the earliest recorded form of Ninian's name is *Nynia*, which could not have resulted in a transcription error from *Uinniau*. Regardless of Ninian's floruit, his cult existed by the early eighth century, and it must have been important or Bede would not have mentioned it in the *HE*.

The primary sources relating to Ninian include two brief mentions by Bede in the *Historia Ecclesiastica*; a verse life of Ninian, *Miracula Nynia Episcopi*, written in the late eighth century; and a prose life, *Vita Niniani*, probably written by Ailred of Rievaulx between 1154 and 1160. John MacQueen (1991) postulates the existence of two lost texts: an original prose life, written in late antiquity, and a later Anglo-Saxon prose life, used by Ailred. Bede (*HE* III.4) states that Ninian was trained in Rome and built a stone church at Whithorn. Bede also said Ninian converted the southern Picts, pre-empting Columba's mission to the northern Picts. Bede's source for this information was probably Pecthelm, the first Anglo-Saxon bishop at Whithorn, who was established there while Bede was writing the *Historia Ecclesiastica*.

Archaeological evidence indicates the presence of a Christian community at Whithorn from the fifth century onwards (Hill 1997). An inscribed memorial stone found on site, dating to the fifth century, includes Christian iconography and a Latin text. The text doesn't mention Ninian, but it does state that Latinus and his daughter established a *sinus* (asylum?) at the site, which might refer to the church. Ninian's church, if it existed, now lies under the medieval structure and other, later ecclesiastical buildings.

All the surviving sources pertaining to Late Antique Britain describe the survival of Christianity and the cult of saints. This is contrary to the view of scholars such as William Frend (1968; 1974; 1979; 1982; 1984; 1992; 1996; 2002; 2004) and Shepard Frere (1966; 1967) that Christianity died out and needed to be reintroduced by missionaries from Ireland and Rome. If Christianity survived in Britain, then the cult of saints probably developed along a similar trajectory as other provinces of the Roman Empire.

Archaeological evidence

Archaeological evidence is frequently employed to corroborate textual sources, and this is true of saints' cults. In Late Antiquity cults were often initially focused around the tombs of saints. As particular cults developed, devotees might enhance the tomb with structural features such as shrines. These shrines sometimes became the nuclei around which churches expanded, with communities in turn developing around them. This process led to many Roman settlements shifting sideways so that in the later Middle Ages they were focused around churches founded over what were once extra-mural cemeteries. These stages can be observed at several sites, such as Tours.

Wilhelm Levison (1941) has compared St Albans and other towns whose medieval centres developed around a church in a Roman extra-mural cemetery, such as Bonn, Xanten, Tours and Cologne. Subsequent archaeological examination has supported the comparison. Excavations by Martin Biddle and Birthe Kjølbye-Biddle have confirmed that the cathedral at St Albans does indeed lie over a Roman extra-mural cemetery (Biddle 1986; Niblett and Thompson 2005). Further evidence indicates possible feasting activity on site corresponding to early Christian rituals celebrating the anniversary of a martyr's death.

So far, however, St. Albans is the only site in Britain where this pattern can be demonstrated in conjunction with near contemporary written attestation. Topographical parallels that have not been examined to the same extent include Great Chesterford (Essex), Ilchester (Somerset) and St Mary de Lode (Gloucester) (Bryant and Heighway 2003; Morris 1989).

Jeremy Knight has presented a cogent argument for the site of the martyrium of Julius and Aaron at a church on a scarp overlooking the River Usk (Knight 2001). The church was set in one of the cemeteries for the legionary fortress located at Caerleon (Legio II Augusta). A charter for a nearby land grant included in the *Book of Llandaff* describes one of the boundaries of the land as the territory of the martyrium of Julius and Aaron. Later documentary evidence suggests that relics of Alban were translated to the church in the twelfth century, which was subsequently rededicated to Alban, and by the eighteenth century, it had ceased being used as a church and had become a barn.

Stephen Matthews has cited St John's church in Chester as the putative location of a Roman martyr's shrine (Matthews 2002). His argument is based primarily on the fact that the church is adjacent to an amphitheatre outside the Roman city walls, a common site of execution. The church could therefore mark the site of the death of a martyr, rather than the grave. This parallels a late antique shrine at the Roman amphitheatre in Tarragona (TED'A 1990).

An archaeological approach

Discussion of archaeological evidence thus far has been limited to methodology conditioned by text. In an article about Anglo-Saxon re-use of prehistoric burial grounds near Yeavering, Richard Bradley suggested that archaeological interpretation and periodisation have been overdetermined by text (Bradley 1987). For example, historians and archaeologists have regarded the year AD 410 as the end of Roman Britain. As a consequence, archaeological literature often refers to anything dated after this point as 'post-Roman'. However, Malcolm Godden has demonstrated that it was Bede, writing three hundred years later, who assigned this date to the end of Roman Britain (Godden 2002).

Therefore, we should ask if the archaeological record matches traditional historical periods. Several factors suggest that it does not. They include evidence of continued occupation at Roman settlements into the fifth and sixth century, such as Verulamium (Frere et al. 1983; Niblett and Thompson 2005; Salway 1981); use of their associated cemeteries from the fourth to the eighth century and later, including sites like Poundbury (Dorset), Cannington (Somerset) and Llandough (Glamorgan) (Farwell and Molleson 1993; Holbrook and Thomas 2005; Rahtz et al. 2000); and the re-use of Iron Age hill forts in southwest Britain from the fourth to the sixth century. Furthermore, the ongoing geophysical survey in the Vale of Pickering, Yorkshire, led by Dominic Powlesland, demonstrates a continuous settlement pattern from Iron Age through to the early medieval period (Powlesland 2003).

An archaeological approach should be determined by what can be asked of material evidence. With the emergence of processual theory, the relevance of textual sources has been neglected. Historical sources should be consulted, if available, provided that they are used critically.

A potential direction for an archaeological approach is the appropriation of prehistoric ritual sites for the location of medieval Christian churches. Some work has already done in this area. David Stocker has found that many churches in the Witham Valley of Lincolnshire were sited at the ends of prehistoric fen causeways marked by votive offerings (Stocker and Everton 2003). Ian Wood and Fred Orton have investigated the Anglo-Saxon stone monument at Bewcastle, which stands in the remains of a Roman Legionary fort that is on top of a pre-Roman ritual site (Orton et al. 2007). Recent investigation conducted by Richard Morris, David Stocker, and Dominic Powlesland at Lastingham (North Yorkshire) has discovered the fabric of a Roman temple in the crypt (Morris *pers. comm.*).

Lastingham offers the opportunity to demonstrate an archaeological approach supported by historical evidence rather than the other way around. Bede describes the foundation of the monastery at Lastingham. Oswald offered a grant of land to be chosen by Cedd for the establishment of a monastery. The chosen site is described as remote, amid steep hills more suited for the habitation of robbers and wild beasts. There is no mention of a Roman temple on site. However, Bede goes on to say that before construction began, Cedd wished to cleanse the site of former crimes through fasting and prayer (*HE* III.23). The 'former crimes' could be a reference to the site's past as a pagan temple.

Conclusion

The use of documentary sources to support archaeological interpretation and vice versa approaches interdisciplinarity. The key to interdisciplinarity is to employ critical methodology of all sources, textual or material. Then one can ask questions that call upon archaeological and historical evidence that cannot be answered exclusively by either. For example, is it possible to detect the grave of a saint whose cult did not become strong enough to attract urban settlement, was stifled, forgotten, arrested or differently configured? Or we might ask how do you distinguish between such a cult and one that simply moved location? Asking such questions and seeking to answer them will help to provide a more comprehensive view of Britain in the early Middle Ages.

Acknowledgements

I would like to thank Caroline Holas-Clark and Zoë Devlin for organising a conference with a theme relevant to my thesis research; as well as Richard Morris and Ian Wood for reading and commenting on early drafts of this paper; and Alex Woolf for the comments on the paper after hearing it presented.

Bibliography

[Bede] 1969. *Ecclesiastical History of the English People*, B. Colgrave and R. Mynors (eds. and trans.), Clarendon Press (Oxford)

Biddle, M. 1986. 'Archaeology, architecture, and the cult of saints in Anglo-Saxon England', in R. Morris (ed.), *The Anglo-Saxon Church: Papers on History, Architecture and Archaeology in Honour of Dr. H.M. Taylor*, Council for British Archaeology (London): 1-31

Bradley, R. 1987. 'Time regained: the creation of continuity', *Journal of the British Archaeological Association,* 140: 1-17

Bryant, R. & Heighway, C. 2003. 'Excavations at St. Mary De Lode Church, Gloucester, 1978-9', *Transactions of the Bristol and Gloucestershire Archaeological Society,* 121: 97-178

Clancy, T.O. 2001. 'The real St. Ninian', *Innes Review,* 52: 1-28

Clark, G. 1999. 'Victricius of Rouen: *Praising the Saints*', *Journal of Early Christian Studies,* 7: 365-399

Clark, G. 2001. 'Translating relics: Victricius of Rouen and fourth-century debate', *Early Medieval Europe,* 10: 161-176

[Constantius] 1920. *Vita Sancti Germani.* in W. Levison (ed.), *Monumenta Germaniae Historica: Scriptores Rerum Merovingicrum,* 7. Hanover.

Dark, K. 2000. *Britain and the End of the Roman Empire,* Tempus (Stroud)

Deanesly, M. & Grosjeans, P. 1959. 'The Canterbury edition of the answers of Pope Gregory I to Augustine', *Journal of Ecclesiastical History,* 10: 1-49

Esmonde Cleary, S. 2001. 'The Roman to medieval transition', in S. James and M. Millett (eds.), *Britons and Romans: Advancing an Archaeological Agenda,* Council for British Archaeology (London): 90-97

Farwell, D.E. & Molleson, T. 1993. *Excavations at Poundbury, 1966-80,* Dorchester, Dorset Natural History and Archaeological Society

Frend, W.H.C. 1968. 'The Christianisation of Roman Britain', in M.W. Barley and R.P.C. Hanson (eds.), *Christianity in Britain, 300-700,* Leicester University Press (Leicester)

Frend, W.H.C. 1974. 'Problems of Late Antiquity', *The Classical Review,* 24: 283-284

Frend, W.H.C. 1979. 'Ecclesia Britannica: prelude or dead end?', *Journal of Ecclesiastical History,* 30: 129-44

Frend, W.H.C. 1982. 'Romano-British Christianity and the West: comparison and contrast', in S.M. Pearce (ed.), *The Early Church in Western Britain and Ireland,* B.A.R., British Series, 102 (Oxford): 5-16

Frend, W.H.C. 1984. *The Rise of Christianity,* Longman and Todd (Darton)

Frend, W.H.C. 1992. 'Pagans, Christians, and 'the Barbarian Conspiracy of AD 367' in Roman Britain', *Britannia,* 23: 121-131

Frend, W.H.C. 1996. *The Archaeology of Early Christianity: A History,* Geoffrey Chapman

Frend, W.H.C. 2002. 'Roman Britain, a failed promise', in R. Sharpe and A. Thacker (eds.), *Local Saints and Local Churches in the Early Medieval West,* Oxford University Press (Oxford)

Frend, W.H.C. 2004. 'Review of M.W. Herren and S.A. Brown (eds.), *Christ in Celtic Christianity. Britain and Ireland from the Fifth to the Tenth Century,* (Woodbridge)', *Journal of Ecclesiastical History,* 55: 139-140

Frere, S. 1966. 'The end of towns in Roman Britain', in J. Wacher, (ed.), *The Civitas Capitals of Roman Britain.* Leicester University (Leicester): 87-100

Frere, S. 1967. *Britannia: A History of Roman Britain.* Routledge (London)

Frere, S., Wilson, M.G. & Society of Antiquaries of London Research Committee. 1983. *Verulamium Excavations,* The Society of Antiquaries of London (London)

Godden, M. 2002. 'The Anglo-Saxons and the Goths: Rewriting the sack of Rome', *Anglo-Saxon England,* 31, 47-68

Handley, M.A. 2001. 'The origins of Christian commemoration in Late Antique Britain', *Early Medieval Europe,* 10: 177-199

Hill, P. 1997. *Whithorn and St. Ninian: the Excavation of a Monastic Town, 1984-91,* Sutton (Stroud)

Holbrook, N. & Thomas, A. 2005. 'An Early-Medieval monastic cemetery at Llandough, Glamorgan: Excavations in 1994', *Medieval Archaeology,* 49: 1-92

Knight, J.K. 2001. 'Britain's other martyrs: Julius, Aaron and Alban at Caerleon', in M. Henig and P. Lindley (eds.), *Alban and St Albans: Roman and Medieval Architecture, Art and Archaeology,* Maney (Leeds): 38-44

Levison, W. 1941. 'St Alban and St Albans', *Antiquity,* 15: 337-59

MacQueen, J. 1991. 'The literary sources for the Life of St. Ninian', in R. Oram and G. Stell (eds.), *Galloway: Land and Lordship,* Scottish Society for Northern Studies (Edinburgh): 17-25

MacQueen, J. 2005. *St. Nynia,* John Donald (Edinburgh)

Matthews, S. 2002. 'St John's church and the early history of Chester', *Journal of the Chester Archaeological Society,* 76: 63-80

Meens, R. 1994. 'A background to Augustine's mission to Anglo-Saxon England', *Anglo-Saxon England*, 23: 5-17

Meens, R. 1996. 'Ritual purity and the influence of Gregory the Great in the early middle ages', *Studies in Church History*, 32: 31-43

Meyer, W. 1904. *Die Legende Des H. Albanus Des Protomartyr Angliae in Texten Vor Beda*, Weidmannsche Buchhandlung (Berlin)

Morris, R. 1989. *Churches in the Landscape*, Dent (London)

Niblett, R. and Thompson, I. 2005. *Alban's Buried Towns: An Assessment of St. Albans' Archaeology up to AD 1600*, Oxbow Books in association with English Heritage (Oxford)

Noble, T.F.X. and Head, T. 1995. *Soldiers of Christ: Saints and Saints' Lives from Late Antiquity and the Early Middle Ages*, Sheed & Ward (London)

O'Sullivan, T. 1978. *The De Excidio of Gildas: Its Authenticity and Date*, E.J. Brill (Leiden)

Orton, F., Wood, I. & Lees, C. 2007. *Fragments of History: Rethinking the Ruthwell and Bewcastle Monuments*, Manchester University Press (Manchester)

Powlesland, D. 2003. *25 Years of Archaeological Research on the Sands and Gravels of Heslerton*, English Heritage (Colchester)

Rahtz, P.A., Hirst, S.M. & Wright, S.M. 2000. *Cannington Cemetery: Excavations 1962-3 of Prehistoric, Roman, Post-Roman, and Later Features at Cannington Park Quarry, near Bridgwater, Somerset*, Society for the Promotion of Roman Studies (London)

Salway, P. 1981. *Roman Britain*, Oxford University Press (Oxford)

Sharpe, R. 2001. 'The Late Antique passion of St Alban', in M. Henig and P. Lindley (eds.), *Alban and St Albans: Roman and Medieval Architecture, Art and Archaeology*, Maney (Leeds)

Sharpe, R. 2002. 'Martyrs and local saints in Late Antique Britain', in A. Thacker and R. Sharpe (eds.), *Local Saints and Local Churches in the Early Medieval West*, Oxford University (Oxford)

Sims-Williams, P. 1983. 'Gildas and the Anglo-Saxons', *Cambridge Medieval Celtic Studies*, 6: 1-30

Stancliffe, C.E. 1999. 'The British church and the mission of St Augustine', in R. Gameson (ed.), *St Augustine and the Conversion of England*, Sutton (Stroud)

Stocker, D.A. and Everton, P. 2003. 'The straight and narrow way: Fenland causeways and the conversion of the landscape in the Witham Valley, Lincolnshire', in M. Carver (ed.), *The Cross Goes North: Processes of Conversion in Northern Europe, AD 300-1300*, York Medieval Press & Boydell Press (Woodbridge, Suffolk)

TED'A 1990. *L'amfiteatre Romà De Tarragona, La Basílica Visigòtica I L'església Romànica*, Taller Escola d'Arqueologia (Tarragona)

Victricius 1985. 'De Laude Sanctorum', in R. Demeulenaere (ed.), *Foebadius. Victricius. Leporius. Vincentius Lerinensis. Evagrius. Rubricius*, Brepols (Turnhout)

Wood, I. 1984. 'The end of Roman Britain: continental evidence and parallels', in M. Lapidge and D.N. Dumville (eds.), *Gildas: New Approaches*, Boydell (Woodbridge)

Wood, I. 1994. 'The mission of Augustine of Canterbury to the English', *Speculum*, 69: 1-17

Wood, I. 1995. 'Pagan religions and superstitions east of the Rhine from the fifth to the ninth century', in G. Ausenda (ed.), *After Empire: Towards an Ethnology of Europe's Barbarians*, Boydell & Brewer (Woodbridge)

Wood, I. 2000a. 'Augustine and Aidan: bureaucrat and charismatic?' in C.D. Dreuille (ed.), *L'église Et La Mission Au Vie Siècle: La Mission D'augustin De Cantorbéry Et Les Églises De Gaule Sous L'impulsion De Grégoire Le Grand Actes Du Colloque D'arles De 1998*, Les Édition du Cerf (Paris)

Wood, I. 2000b. 'Some historical re-identifications and the Christianization of Kent', in G. Armstrong (ed.), *Christianizing Peoples and Converting Individuals*, Brepols (Turnhout)

Alcuin of York on Wisdom and Mary: texts and buildings

Sarah Jane Boss

Introduction[1]

In his delightful and fascinating poem, 'On the Saints of the Church of York',[2] Alcuin (*c*.732-804) records the building of a new church in the city, consecrated by Archbishop Albert in 779. On Albert's instructions, Alcuin himself, with Eanbald, another of Albert's pupils, undertook the construction of the church, which he describes as

> A lofty building, raised on solid piers
> Supporting rounded arches, and within
> Fine pannelling and windows made it bright,
> A lovely sight, with gleaming cloisters round
> And many upper rooms beneath the roofs
> And thirty altars variously decked.
> (ll. 1508-1513; Allott 1974, 164)

This large and lavish building was dedicated to 'alma Sophia' (l.1518), a title which signifies the figure of holy Wisdom.

The location of this church is unknown, but attempts to reconstruct the topography of Anglo-Saxon York have given rise to at least two proposals as to where it might have been.[3] The proposal that is of particular interest for the present paper is that put forward by Christopher Norton, who suggests that the Sophia church may have occupied the site where the thirteenth-century Minster chapter house stands,[4] and that, like the chapter house, it would have been built to an octagonal plan. Norton points out that the chapter house, which stands to the north of the Minster and is connected to it only by an L-shaped vestibule, is on a different alignment from the main body of the Minster (Fig. 1). He writes:

> the misalignment is not the result of an accident. It was known and indeed designed into the chapter-house from the start, as is evident from the fact that the inner face of the entrance bay is aligned with the rest of the chapter-house so as to form a regular octagon, whereas the exterior face of the same entrance bay (which is unquestionably part of the same build) is aligned square on to the vestibule, and thus to the rest of the Minster. The thick wall of the entrance bay largely conceals the fact that it is not rectangular, but wedge-shaped, to compensate for the change of alignment. The entrance bay was carefully and deliberately designed from the beginning to take account of the fact that the chapter-house was being constructed on a special alignment. ... The hypothesis presents itself that the chapter-house was built over, and perpetuated the memory of a much earlier building laid out on the Anglo-Saxon alignment [of the Minster complex as a whole]. If so, it must have been a very significant structure. Could it have been the church of the Alma Sophia?
> (Norton 1998, 14-15)

In this paper, I shall consider Norton's suggestion concerning the chapter house, from the point of view of both archaeological and textual evidence, because the idea that Alcuin's church of Alma Sophia may have been an octagon is exceptionally interesting for the history of an important motif in Catholic theology and devotion. From the high Middle Ages onwards, the Virgin Mary was strongly associated with the scriptural figure of Holy Wisdom. The origin of this association is not known, but the earliest surviving liturgical text that includes a Wisdom lection for a Marian feast was written by Alcuin. Moreover, centrally planned buildings – and, arguably, octagons in particular – were frequently dedicated to the Blessed Virgin. So if Wisdom was the dedication of an octagonal church built by Alcuin, it would seem that he combined Marian and Sapiential motifs in a building, just as he combined them in liturgy. This in turn suggests new directions for investigation into the origin of the identification of Mary with Wisdom.

A previous structure

Let us consider, then, the possibility that there was an earlier structure on the site of the present chapter house. As we have seen, Norton's main argument for this is the fact that the alignment of the chapter house is slightly at variance with the alignment of the Minster church, and that a deliberate correction has been made for this. At the same time, 'the north-east face of the chapter-house aligns more or less with Minster Yard ..., and the north-west face with the base line of the 7th-century square enclosure' (Norton 1998, 15). Thus, it seems at least possible that there had been an Anglo-Saxon building on the site, of which enough survived after the Norman

---

[1] Christopher Norton and Jon Cannon kindly commented on an earlier draft of this paper, and have enabled me to improve it considerably. I am indebted to both of them for the trouble they have taken. Since I have not followed their advice on all counts, I am certainly responsible for the failings that remain.
[2] English translation (abridged) in Allott (1974, 157-167).
[3] One of these is contained in Morris (1986). Morris suggests that the Sophia church was on the site subsequently occupied by Holy Trinity Priory. This view will not be discussed here.
[4] For evidence for the dating of the chapter house to the 1280s, see Brown (2003, 51-5).

Conquest for it to be rehabilitated for use as a chapter house.

All this is plausible, but we should not entirely rule out the possibility that the misalignment is the result of an accident. Norton does not give measurements of the relevant angles, but – from the plan he provides and from the experience of standing at the site – the alignment of the chapter house with the Anglo-Saxon enclosure does not seem to be very much better than its alignment with the existing church. Moreover, the fact that the wedge-shaped entrance wall is original does not make it impossible that this device was put into the plan after construction work on the chapter house had already begun, to correct for a misalignment that had occurred in the initial stages of building. On the other hand, if, as seems to be the case, the building was constructed as a single piece, rather than in sections, then Norton's proposal that the alignment was deliberate from the start is more likely to be true.

Norton also points out that at the north end of the east wall of the north transept – which was built in the early thirteenth century, some decades before the chapter house – there is a wide doorway, apparently for ceremonial purposes, which leads out into the chapter house yard. If there were an earlier building on the site of the chapter house, then the presence of such a building would account for the existence of this doorway (Norton 1998, 15). The unusual L-shape of the passageway connecting the church and chapter house also suggests that, for some reason, the situations of both church and chapter house, respectively, were already fixed.[5]

In a more recent paper, Norton draws attention to the fact that 'the earliest capitular seal of York Minster, which probably dates to around the time of the establishment of the Dean and Chapter as an independent body c.1090 ... depicts Saint Peter, the Minster's patron saint, holding in one hand a miniature building', which 'looks like a cylindrical pepper-pot with a steeply-pointed roof' (Norton forthcoming; illustration in Salter 1929, n.56.). This seems to suggest that a centrally planned building formed part of the Minster complex at the end of the eleventh century.

So, although Norton's evidence does not amount to a conclusive argument for the present chapter house occupying the site of an earlier building, his hypothesis does provide an explanation for some features of the existing buildings, and, as this paper will try to show, it invites us to consider how the history of a building might combine with textual evidence to shed light on a question in the history of theology, namely, the origins of the identification of the Virgin Mary with Holy Wisdom.

---

[5] Jon Cannon (pers. comm.) has pointed out that the doorway in the north transept could have been built as the ceremonial entranceway for the archbishop from his palace, and suggests that the L-shaped plan is a stronger reason for thinking that there may have been an earlier building on the site of the chapter house.

The Marian rotunda

Wisdom and polygony

Norton has suggested that the Anglo-Saxon octagonal church which may have preceded the Minster chapter house could have been the same church which Alcuin says was dedicated to 'Alma Sophia'. The term 'Alma Sophia' is a mixture of Greek and Latin – *Sophia* being the Greek for Wisdom, and *alma* a Latin word meaning 'dear', or 'beloved'.[6] Ruth Meyers, in a paper on Alcuin's Mass in honour of Holy Wisdom, suggested that the adjective *alma* should perhaps not be understood as part of the Church's official dedication, but as a term expressing Alcuin's own love of Wisdom (Meyers 1995, 52). This suggestion is supported by references to *Titulus Agiae Sophiae* in a calendar written at Prüm in the middle of the ninth century, evidently referring to the church of Archbishop Albert (Norton forthcoming, citing Bullough 2002). We shall return to this topic later on. For the present, what matters is the fact that Wisdom was the object of a church dedication. Norton writes:

> Given the rarity of a dedication to the Alma Sophia, it is particularly interesting that a centrally-planned church dedicated to the Divine Wisdom (Agia Sophia or Sancta Sapientia) was under construction in the 750s at Benevento. It seems to have been completed about 765, and could well have come to the attention of Archbishop Aelberht and Alcuin when they visited Rome before 767 (Norton 1998, 15).

Norton implies that this visit of Alcuin and Albert's to Benevento could have influenced their own building of a centrally planned church which was dedicated to Holy Wisdom, namely, the church which would have stood on the site of the present chapter house. So, what if Albert and Alcuin decided that a centrally planned building was indeed the most appropriate form for their new church, and that the octagon was a suitable form for a church with this dedication? This is the hypothesis which will now be pursued.

In a paper on the icongraphy of an illumination from Guyart des Moulins' *Bible Historiale* (c.1420), Pamela Tudor-Craig argues that 'centrally planned buildings, especially chapter houses, of the High Middle Ages were specifically designed to attract the guidance of Wisdom' during the deliberations that took place in these buildings

---

[6] The use of Greek terms in insular literature deserves more study than it has so far received. The Lindisfarne Gospels use Greek titles and names for the four evangelists, which may be relevant to the use of the term *Sophia* by Alcuin and by Acca (see below). Another relevant text may be John Scotus Eriugena's poem *Aulae Sidereae*, which was composed for the construction or dedication of Charles the Bald's church at Compiègne in 877. The church was dedicated to the Virgin Mary, and was supposed to be a copy of Charlemagne's chapel at Aix-la-Chapelle, the construction of which had been influenced by Alcuin. Commentators think that the building at Compiègne was octagonal, partly because the poem gives particular prominence to the number 'eight'. The poem also contains many Greek terms, including 'Sophia'. See Foussard (1971); Vieillard-Troïekouroff (1971); Herren (1987).

(Tudor-Craig 2002, 110). This is because of the Platonic notion that the circle is the perfect geometrical form, and that it is this form which most clearly resembles the character of divine Wisdom – a belief which was undoubtedly widespread for many hundreds of years. So, according to Tudor-Craig, the reason why the polygon was favoured as a plan for chapter houses is that it is almost circular, and thus would assist the conduct of wise counsel. If she is correct, then her evidence lends support to Norton's hypothesis that an octagonal church dedicated to Wisdom may have preceded the present chapter house at York Minster. However, there is a certain weakness in her argument, since it depends upon the notion that the builders of these chapter houses made no distinction between circular and polygonal constructions. She is not the only author to make this assumption,[7] but I think it needs to be treated with caution. It may well be the case that the casual chronicler describes a polygonal building as 'circular' or 'nearly circular'; but it is certain (as Tudor-Craig implicitly recognises) that the people who commissioned sacred buildings attributed great symbolic importance to number and shape, so that the difference between a circle and an eight-sided construction would be clearly registered by them; and the masons who constructed the buildings would necessarily have been well aware of the differences in planning and stone-dressing that would be required for a circular, as distinct from an octagonal, building. In the later Middle Ages, the requirement for a large quantity of glazing would have made a round building impractical in many circumstances, and a polygonal building might well have served as a substitute. But even then a decision would have to be made as to how many sides the substitute should possess: six, or eight, or ten (as in the chapter house at Lincoln Cathedral)? It is reasonable to suppose that that decision might be determined in part by considerations of sacred symbolism; so we cannot presume that a polygon is just a circle *manqué*. This raises the question as to whether or not the octagon as such might be particularly appropriate for a building dedicated to Wisdom. Before addressing this question directly, however, we must consider what is known about other centrally planned churches in general, and about octagonal ones in particular.

Let us begin with the centrally planned churches of Anglo-Saxon England. The evidence comes from texts, rather than archaeology, and it is not very great, but it does suggest that centrally planned churches were often dedicated to the Virgin Mary. Those at Abingdon and Hexham are examples of this (Gem 1983, 137-8), and the practice of using central planning for Marian spaces seems to have continued in England during the later Middle Ages (Cannon 2006). Ought we, then, to consider the possibility that an earlier octagonal building on the site of the York chapter house was dedicated to Mary?

Marian architecture

The present Lady chapel of York Minster is the fourteenth-century eastern chapel, beyond the high altar. Before the construction of the present eastern arm of the Minster, the principle chapel in honour of the Virgin Mary may have been the free-standing chapel of St. Mary and the Holy Angels, which stood to the north of the nave (see Fig. 1). This chapel was founded by Archbishop Roger of Pont-l'Evêque, probably in the late 1170s (Thompson 1947, 63-5), and seems to have been completed in the fourteenth century under the direction of Archbishop John of Thoresby (r.1352-73), who was also responsible for the eastern extension of the quire (Browne 1847, 180; Brown 2003, 137-9). The chapel fell into decay after the Reformation, and today, all that can be seen of it is a doorway in the north wall of the nave, which would have given access to the chapel from the main church.[8] In the nineteenth century, John Browne excavated a small part of the chapel, and his findings indicate that it was orientated on a north-east / south-west axis, on a substantially different alignment from that of the Minster proper (Browne 1847, 181). This raises two further questions: Was there a Lady Chapel before Archbishop Roger's building? And why was the Chapel of St. Mary and the Holy Angels on a different alignment from that of the Minster?

Christopher Norton suggests that the chapel stood on the site of a chapel dedicated to St. Mary from the Anglo-Saxon period, one which Alcuin designates as 'aula Christigenitricis' in his poem *On the Saints of the Church of York* (l.1599)[9] (Norton 1998, 14; Allott 1974, 166). The chapel's location on an earlier site would account for the fact that its alignment differs from that of the Minster, and Norton argues persuasively that its alignment may well correspond to that of the earlier Anglo-Saxon cathedral and its enclosure.

At other sites, it has been suggested that the reason why a smaller free-standing chapel was placed on a different alignment from the larger church at its side was in order to indicate that the chapel, although smaller, was of some particular importance. For example, at Walsingham, the Holy House was aligned slightly differently from the priory church on whose north side it stood, and it was the Holy House which was the more sacred place and the

---

[7] Tudor-Craig takes her lead from Richard Krautheimer (1969: 115-150).

[8] Norton (1998, 11) suggests that there would have been a passageway here, linking the two buildings.
[9] To a mariologist, the title 'Christi genitrix' – the Latin equivalent of the Greek *Christotókos* – looks strange, because, following the Nestorian controversy (which was resolved after the Council of Ephesus in 431), the Eastern churches ceased using this title for Mary, because of its association with Nestorius's heresy. Instead, they used only the title *Theotókos*, which is translated into Latin as 'Deigenitrix', 'Deipara', or, most often, 'Mater Dei'. In the later Middle Ages and early modern period in the West, these latter titles were used very frequently, and – as far as I can tell from my own reading – 'Christigenitrix' was not used at all. During the earlier and high Middle Ages, however – for example, in some British and Carolingian sources – 'Christotokos' seems to be used occasionally. Alcuin uses the Greek *Christotókos* – which can be applied both to Mary and to others – in contrast to *Theotókos*, which can be used only of Mary. See below.

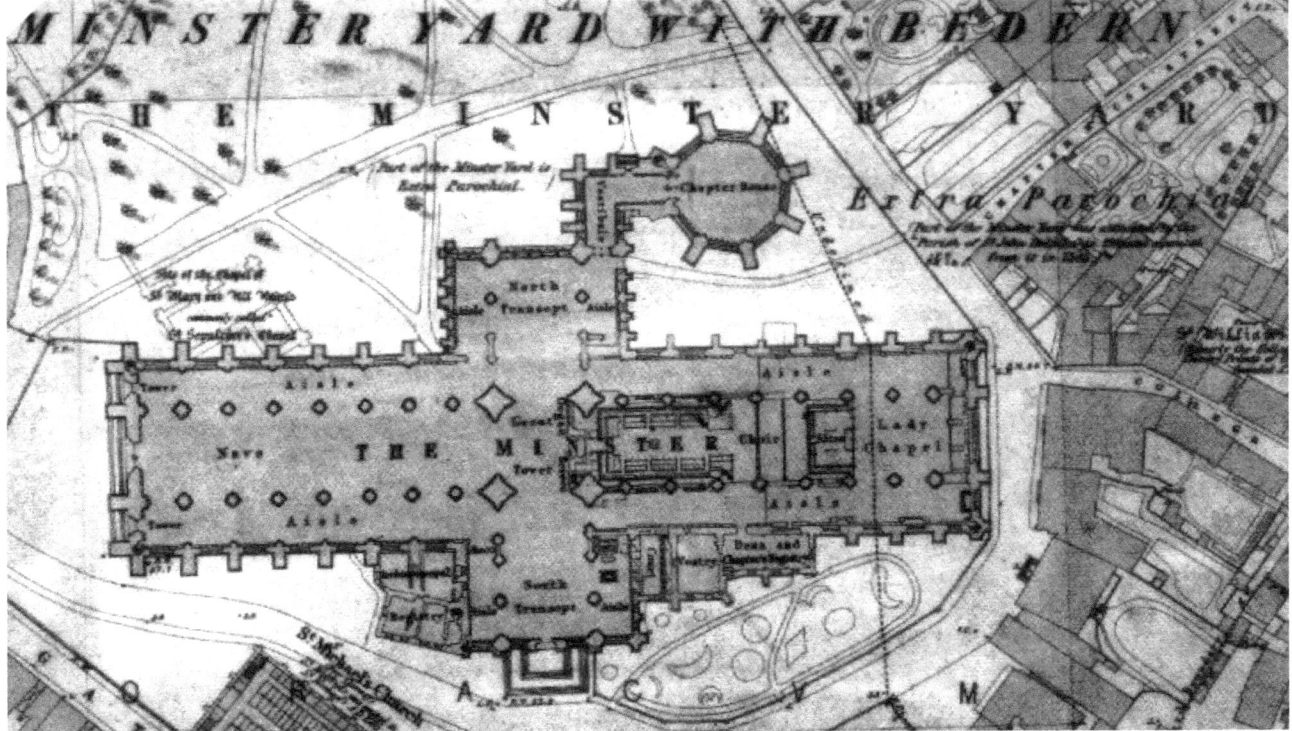

Fig. 1. Map of York Minster in 1852, showing the foundations of the chapel of St Mary and the Angels to the west of the North Transept. Copyright Ordnance Survey.

object of pilgrimage.[10] At Burford (Oxfordshire), a free-standing chapel in honour of St. Anne and the Virgin Mary stood on the south side of the parish church, at a slight angle to the larger building, until the fifteenth century, when it was in effect incorporated into the main church building as the Lady Chapel. Nothing is known of the history of the chapel of St. Anne and St. Mary, but it seems reasonable to suggest that at Burford, as at Walsingham, the fact that the chapel was free-standing and on a different alignment from the church may have been because the chapel was on an earlier site that had been preserved because it was of some particular cultic significance. All this could be true of the chapel of St. Mary and the Holy Angels at York.

However, there is another observation which needs to be factored in to these considerations. According to the work of Richard Krautheimer, a dedication of the form 'St. Mary and other heavenly beings' (i.e., angels, saints, martyrs, etc.) marks a whole family of churches that were centrally planned, dating from late antiquity until the high middle ages ('Sancta Maria Rotunda', in Krautheimer 1969, 107-114). Now, at York we have a centrally planned chapter house, possibly on the site of an earlier building, together with another chapel dedicated to St. Mary and the Holy Angels. Is it possible that there was once an octagonal chapel dedicated to St. Mary and the Holy Angels, and that this started to be used for chapter meetings? If so, then, in the light of this new use, it may have been determined in the twelfth century to build a separate chapel in honour of St. Mary and the Holy Angels. This would enable the chapter to hold its meetings in a separate space, so that they would not impede, or be impeded by, the various liturgies and devotions that were conducted in the Mary chapel. The choice of site and alignment for the new chapel may have been determined by the fact that an earlier chapel had indeed been built on ground which was by then to the north of the Minster nave.[11]

Krautheimer suggests that the reason why centrally planned buildings were often dedicated to Mary was that this was the form of the church which housed the Virgin's tomb in Jerusalem, and that the other churches were constructed in imitation of this. Her tomb was the place from which, according to tradition, she was assumed into Heaven to become the leading figure of the celestial hosts, and Krautheimer argues that this would account for why it is that the dedications of Marian rotundas so often include a band of other heavenly beings along with St. Mary herself. It has been suggested by Nicholas Dawton that the thirteenth-century chapter house at York Minster is in some sense a shrine to the Virgin in a form that deliberately resembles her tomb (Dawton 1990). His argument is highly speculative, but we should not rule out the possibility that not only the ground-plan, but also its symbolic meaning, would have

---

[10] It is possible that the building of Lady chapels to the north of the main church building (e.g., in the Augustinian Priory – now the cathedral – at Bristol) was in imitation of the arrangement at Walsingham.

[11] It is interesting to note that the popular name for the Chapel of St. Mary and the Angels was St. Sepulchre. The reason for this is not known, but the Church of the Holy Sepulchre in Jerusalem was centrally planned, and the central planning of many European churches was a conscious imitation of this. Thus, the official and popular titles of the free-standing chapel to the north of the Minster nave were both associated with centrally planned buildings.

been retained if the new chapter house was built on the site of an earlier sacred building. If we follow Norton's hypothesis that the chapter house might occupy a site which was previously the site of a church dedicated to Holy Wisdom, then in this case also there would be continuity of dedication in the sense that the chapter meeting would seek the guidance of Wisdom in its deliberations. It remains to be shown, however, that we do not necessarily have to choose between a dedication to Holy Wisdom and a dedication to the Virgin Mary, and why the octagonal form may be a way of expressing a theological teaching that is both Marian and Sapiential.

Wisdom and Mary in the later Middle Ages[12]

In the Old Testament, Wisdom seems to be an aspect of God. There are a number of passages in which the personified figure of Wisdom speaks, calling humanity to follow in her ways, and describing her own relationship to God and creation. For example, in Proverbs 8, we read, 'Does not wisdom call, does not understanding raise her voice? On the heights beside the way, in the paths she takes her stand' (vv.1-2, RSV). Wisdom herself says, 'Take my instruction instead of silver, and knowledge rather than choice gold; for wisdom is better than jewels, and all that you may desire cannot compare with her' (vv.10-11, RSV). Further on, Wisdom reveals herself as a figure of cosmic significance, when she says, 'The Lord created me at the beginning of his way, the first of his acts of old' (v.22, RSV). She goes on to explain that she was established before the beginning of the earth – indeed, before anything was created – and that she was present with God, 'like a master craftsman' (v.30, RSV),[13] when he marked out the earth's foundations. Thus, the moral and natural orders of the world have the same origin. Wisdom is involved in the making of the natural world, implying that those who follow her teaching will be aligning themselves with the very foundations of the cosmos.

In the New Testament, Wisdom is identified with Jesus Christ. St. Paul, in his first Letter to the church at Corinth, writes, 'Christ is our Wisdom' (1 Cor.1:24, 30), and speaks of the world as having been created through Christ (1 Cor.8:6). Likewise, in the prologue to John's Gospel, Christ is called 'the Word' – in Greek, *ho logos* – who, 'in the beginning', was not only present with God, but was even identical with God, and through whom all things were made (Jn.1:1-3). The figure of the Logos here seems to be the same as Wisdom, or Sophia.

However, in the Western church during the Middle Ages, Old Testament texts referring to Holy Wisdom were commonly used in liturgies for feasts of the Blessed Virgin Mary. The passages that were most widely used were Proverbs 8:22-31; Proverbs 9:1-5; and Ecclesiasticus 24:5-31 (Vulgate).[14] We shall go on to consider the latter two passages in more detail in a moment. Because these passages were used in Marian liturgies, their accounts of Wisdom came to be applied to Mary as well as to Christ. She too was seen as more desirable than jewels and sweeter than honey; she too was present – at least in the mind of God – before the creation of the world. Some theologians – especially, perhaps, the followers of John Duns Scotus (1265-1308) – contended that God had intended from all eternity to become incarnate in Jesus Christ: indeed, that this was part of the purpose for which the world had been created. God made the world in order to bring it to fulfillment and glorification, and the incarnation of the Word of God in Jesus of Nazareth was the means and highest manifestation of this glorification. Now, given that the means of the incarnation was to be a virginal conception by a particular woman from whom Christ would take his humanity, it was argued that the mother of God incarnate must have been predestined to this unique dignity in the same act by which God ordained the incarnation itself. If God determined from all eternity that the Word of God would become incarnate from the Blessed Virgin Mary, then Mary herself must have been similarly predestined to be the Mother of God. Thus, there was indeed some sense in which Mary was present with God from eternity. This particular Mariological theme, however, is not explicitly developed until the later Middle Ages. What, then, was the origin of the use of Wisdom texts in Marian liturgies?

Mary and Wisdom in liturgical texts

Let us ask this question more generally: what is the origin of the Western church's association between Mary and Wisdom? This question includes consideration of where and when this association began, and of what was the occasion of its origin – liturgy, or devotion, or theological discussion, perhaps? What was the implicit or explicit rationale for associating Mary with Wisdom? If Norton's suggestion that there was an Anglo-Saxon octagonal church dedicated to Wisdom is correct, then this might provide a clue along the path towards answering some of these questions. For, as we have seen, most, if not all, of the other circular or polygonal churches that are known about from Anglo-Saxon England were dedicated to the Virgin Mary. Furthermore, it seems likely that the earliest surviving witness to the use of a Wisdom text in Marian liturgy comes from Alcuin. So, was Alcuin's church of 'alma Sophia' a building which deliberately incorporated a symbol of the Virgin Mary, just as his Marian liturgy deliberately incorporated a text describing Holy Wisdom? If so, then why? What was the meaning of this association in Anglo-Saxon England, and might the church's octagonal form help us to answer that question?

Let us turn, then, to look at the earliest use of Wisdom texts in Marian liturgies. Ecclesiasticus 24:11-20 is found

---

[12] This section recapitulates work that I have published elsewhere. See Boss (2000, 139-140); Boss (2004, 111-112 and 114-115).
[13] The Vulgate has, 'cum eo eram cuncta componens'.

[14] vv. 24:3-22 RSV, with significant textual differences from the Vulgate.

in a Latin lectionary of the seventh century, the *Comes* of Würtzburg, for feasts of virgin saints (Catta 1961, 693-4). It begins with the line in which Wisdom says, 'et in omnibus requiem quaesivi', that is, 'and in all things I sought rest', and goes on to speak of her being established in Sion. A consecrated virgin was understood to be a bride of Christ, and we might suppose that the association between the virgin saint and Wisdom is derived from the Gospel parable of the wise virgins, who keep their lamps ready as they await the bridegroom. The voice of Wisdom would thus be the voice of Christ, to whom the virgin saint devoted her life. However, one modern commentator, Etienne Catta, suggests that this reading is intended to be heard as the voice of the virgin herself, who, in choosing a holy life, has sought the place of her repose away from the bustle of the world (Catta 1961, 693). Clearly, we do not have to choose one interpretation or the other here: either or both can be heard. But there is evidence that the reading was indeed intended to be heard as the voice of the virgin saint, rather than eternal Wisdom, or Christ, since verse 14 (vv.9-10 RSV) is omitted from the seventh-century lectionary. This verse reads: 'From the beginning, before the ages, I was created, and until the age to come I shall not cease to be, and in his holy dwelling place I ministered before him.' If Wisdom's words were placed in the mouth of Christ, there would be no problem about this verse being used, since Christ is eternal. The fact that this verse is left out, suggests that Wisdom's words are placed primarily in the mouth of the saint whose feast is being celebrated.

In the latter half of the seventh century, the feasts of the Annunciation and of the Virgin's Nativity and Assumption were officially introduced into Rome, principally by the Syrian Pope Sergius (Frénaud 1961, 175), though it seems unlikely that they had not been widely celebrated in the West before this date. It is not certain what lections were used for these Masses, although in later centuries, the Wisdom texts that I have already mentioned were frequently employed both for Masses and for the divine office on the feasts of the Nativity and Assumption, and, later, of the Virgin's Conception. So it is not unlikely that a lection which previously had been used for the feast days of virgin saints was used again for feasts of the Virgin Mary.

When we come to look at Alcuin's own liturgical references to Wisdom, we have something of an embarrassment of riches. It is well known that he had a great devotion to Holy Wisdom, and that his epitaph included the words, 'Alcuin was my name. I always loved wisdom.' He composed texts for at least one mass in honour of Wisdom, and he seems to have used Wisdom texts as the lections for masses in honour of the Virgin Mary. Of particular interest here is the Mass that is headed, 'Mass of Saint Mary on Saturday' (*PL* 101: 455B-D). The lection that Alcuin designates for this mass begins at Ecclesiasticus 24:14 – that is to say, with the very verse that was excluded from the Mass of virgin saints, in which Wisdom says that she was present from before the world existed, that she will not cease to be, and that she ministered in the Lord's holy dwelling place.

So how are we to read this? The obvious first thought is that Alcuin wants the hearer to understand that it is Mary, in whose honour the Mass is celebrated, who is speaking about herself in these exalted terms. However, I suggest that we would do well to start by thinking along lines other than this one. I have already mentioned that Wisdom is identified with Christ in the New Testament, and Ruth Meyers points out that, elsewhere, Alcuin identifies Wisdom with all three persons of the Trinity, and suggests that, in the Mass in honour of Wisdom, Alcuin associates Wisdom with both Christ and the Holy Spirit (Meyers 1995, 53-6). Meyers draws particular attention to the prayer 'super populum' (presumably a closing prayer), in which God is asked to 'prepare a dwelling-place in our hearts for *agia sophia*', that is, for Holy Wisdom, who – as in the case of the church built by Bishop Albert – is named in Greek, rather than Latin. This use of language may refer directly to the dedication of the Sophia church (Norton forthcoming, citing Bullough 2002). Meyers correctly points out that the characteristic of 'indwelling' suggests an appeal for the Holy Spirit, the Third Person of the Blessed Trinity. St. Paul had said that the human body is a Temple of the Holy Spirit, and the notion of the Spirit indwelling the Christian soul is a common one in Patristic and Mediaeval authors. However, this should not lead us to overlook another motif, namely, that of Christ, the Second Person of the Trinity, being likewise present within the soul. From the time of Origen (c.185-254) onwards, there are Christian authors who say that the soul should be like Mary in conceiving Christ spiritually and bearing him to the world.[15] Augustine says that all Christians should be Mothers of Christ (O'Carroll 1982, 65), or Christbearers; and Alcuin, in a piece of theological writing, says that only Mary is the *Theotókos*, or 'Mother of God' – that is to say, only Mary is the mother of God incarnate – but that others have been *Xristotókoi*, or mothers of Christ (*PL* 101:46D-47A). Thus, Mary is simultaneously the exceptional and exemplary type of the Christ-bearing soul.

Mary herself is often compared to the Jerusalem Temple in the work of Patristic and Mediaeval authors, because God incarnate dwelt in her, as the Lord dwelt in his tabernacle on Mount Sion. For example, a Coptic homily attributed to St. Basil of Caesaraea speaks of the Temple as having been built after the pattern of the creation of the world, and ends by saying that every Christian is a temple of God, that Christ is the Temple of God, but that Mary is the true Temple, because the Lord incarnate dwelt within her (Budge 1910, 257). In very different vein, St. Ambrose, apparently warning against particular manifestations of Marian devotion, says, 'Mary is the temple of God, not the God of the temple' (O'Carroll 1982, 21).

---

[15] Origen writes: 'Every virginal, incorrupt soul, having conceived of the Holy Sirit to engender the will of the Father, is the mother of Christ.' Quoted in O'Carroll (1982, 274).

At this point, it is important to bring in another of the Wisdom texts mentioned above, namely, Proverbs 9:1: 'Wisdom has built herself a house, she has hewn her seven pillars.' This text is routinely applied to the Virgin Mary and the incarnation. Wisdom is understood to be Christ, and the house which he has built is the Virgin in whose womb he dwelt and whose flesh and blood became his own. For example, an Anglo-Saxon author of the eleventh century, Eadmer of Canterbury (d.1124), wrote a *Treatise on the Conception of Saint Mary*, in which he uses the fact that Mary is 'Wisdom's house', that is, the Temple of the Word of God, as an argument for her being conceived without original sin (Eadmer 1904).

Against this background, then, I suggest that, when Alcuin used Ecclesiasticus 24:14, 'ab initio ante saeculum creata sum', as the lection for a Mass in honour of the Virgin Mary, he intended us to understand Wisdom as Christ, and the line, 'in his holy dwelling-place I ministered before him' ('et in habitatione sancta coram ipso ministravi') as a reference to the Blessed Virgin Mary: she is the Lord's holy dwelling-place.

Furthermore, there are two small pieces of evidence from Anglo-Saxon England which might be interpreted as indicating that Christ as Holy Wisdom was seen most particularly as the son of Mary, that is to say, as the Word of God specifically in his human incarnation. The first of these pieces is textual, and comes from Symeon of Durham's *Historia Regum*. For the date 740, there is a note of the death and burial of Bishop (subsequently Saint) Acca. It is also recorded that, when his remains were translated – some time after 1050 – there was found among the relics 'an object shaped like an altar ... and made of two boards joined by silver nails. It carried an inscription reading ALMAE TRINITATI. AGIÆ SOPHIÆ. SANCTÆ MARIÆ.' Although this passage is probably a later interpolation, it is not at all unlikely that such an object had really been found (Bailey 1974, 141). So here we have a dedication to the three Persons of the Trinity, followed by Holy Wisdom, followed by Saint Mary. If Wisdom is Christ, then he is appropriately situated between the heavenly Trinity, of whom he is a member, and the woman who gave him his flesh on earth. If we understand the dedication to designate Christ in both his natures, human and divine, then the divine nature is signified by 'Almae Trinitati', and the human by 'Agiae Sophiae'. And there is reason to think that this is indeed how the Acca dedication should be read, not only because it makes sense theologically, but also because of the second piece of evidence, which is a manuscript illumination. Perhaps it is not too fanciful to associate Acca's set of four persons[16] (Father, Son, Holy Spirit, and Mary) under five guises (Father/Son/Spirit, Holy Wisdom and Mary) with the well known eleventh-century 'Quinity' illumination from Winchester (BL ms, Cotton Titus D.xxvii, f.75v; Clayton 1990, Plate VIII; see Fig. 2), and illuminations from the ninth-century Utrecht Psalter on which the Winchester illumination seems to be based.[17] For in the Quinity, the Virgin and Child are shown with all three Persons of the Trinity – Father and Son in human form, and the Spirit in the form of a dove. Thus, there are five figures – Father-as-man, Son-as-man, Spirit-as-dove, Virgin Mary and Son-as-child – standing for four persons – Father, Son, Spirit and Mary. So Christ as the son of Mary (as distinct from the eternal Word/Son of the Trinity) in effect corresponds to the Agia Sophia of Acca's altar dedication. When we map the Acca dedication onto the Winchester Quinity (and its artistic predecessors), therefore, we find that Holy Wisdom, 'Agia Sophia', is God incarnate, bound to the woman who gave him flesh.

Having said this, we should be wary of being too quick to distinguish between that which is Marian (that is, pertaining to the Virgin Mary) and that which is dominical (that is, pertaining to Christ the Lord) during the early and Mediaeval periods. Modern liturgists, and other scholars influenced by modern and Protestant understandings of the nature of Christianity, like to mark out clear-cut boundaries between that which is 'really' about Christ, and that which is 'really' about Mary: for example, the feast of Candlemas, which historically has been called both 'the Purification of the Virgin Mary' and 'the Presentation of Christ in the Temple', is nowadays designated as 'dominical' rather than 'Marian', which is

Fig. 2. The Winchester Quinity, BL ms, Cotton Titus D. xxvii, f.75v. Reproduced with kind permission of the British Library.

---

[16] In Catholic and Orthodox theology, since the Council of Chalcedon (451), it is taught that Christ is one Person in two natures. The Person is the eternal Word, or Son, of God – the Second Person of the Blessed Trinity. Christ has two *natures*, human and divine, but he is not a human *person*.

[17] References for the mss. and the scholarship concerning them are given in Clayton (1990, 166).

to say that it is the feast only of the Presentation of Christ. And historians of liturgy often try to map this clear distinction back onto earlier centuries; but to Mediaeval thinkers, for a thousand years, Mary's uniquely intimate connection with her divine Son meant that these boundaries were fuzzy and flexible. We can see an example of this precisely in relation to the text of Ecclesiasticus 24:14, 'From the beginning, before the world, I was created'. In 853, Haymon, Bishop of Halberstadt, preached on this text as applied to Mary. His homily explains that the Wisdom of God took flesh of the Virgin, but that it is not unsuitable to apply this text to the Mother of God herself, since the Wisdom of God was created from her, 'that through her the Son of God might be created without human concupiscence, to ransom human nature' (*PL* 118:765D).

Mary and Wisdom in sacred buildings

So far, then, we have seen that centrally planned churches were often dedicated to the Virgin Mary, and that Alcuin associated Mary with Holy Wisdom. It has also been argued that Alcuin's association of Mary with Wisdom was concerned primarily with her function as Godbearer, and thus as bearer of Holy Wisdom, but also, in virtue of that, with her own contracting of the qualities proper to her divine Son. All this suggests why it is that a church dedicated to Holy Wisdom might have been constructed to a central plan, i.e., in a characteristically Marian form, and so lends plausibility to Norton's hypothesis concerning the origin of the York chapter house octagon.

There are further considerations which add weight to the idea that a building consecrated to Wisdom would have Marian characteristics. It has already been pointed out that the Blessed Virgin, as the dwelling-place of God, was routinely associated with the Temple in Jerusalem. She was also, and from equally early times, associated with the Church as a mystical body. Patristic and Mediaeval authors present her as a type of the Church – perhaps initially because the Church had taken over the previous function of the Temple as the Tabernacle of God. We should perhaps consider the possibility that this sense of Mary as Temple and Church extended to particular church buildings. Thus, whilst a given church may be Marian in the sense of being a shrine which houses the Blessed Virgin Mary, a church may also be Marian in the sense of being a stone embodiment of her, which houses the presence of Christ. That is to say, the church building shares in the identity of the Blessed Virgin, because it, like her, is a shrine of her Son. The wall of the chapter house at York Minster bears the legend, 'Ut rosa flos florum, sic est domus ista domorum': As the rose is the flower of flowers, so is this the house of houses. Several commentators have correctly observed that the rose is an emblem of the Virgin Mary; but most of them have not spotted that the word 'house' also signifies the Mother of God, and that the 'house of houses' is precisely what she is.

So is there any reason for thinking that an octagonal building would express this Marian symbol with particular clarity? It is not immediately obvious that this is so. In Patristic thought, the number eight has several sacred resonances (for example, the day of Christ's Circumcision is the eighth day following his birth), but most especially, it is associated with the Resurrection. The Resurrection, which takes place on the first day of the week, is said to occur on the eighth day, thus surpassing even the sacred seventh day of the first creation. This may account for the octagonal form of a number of early Christian churches, and it is probably for this reason that baptistries are often octagonal: the new Christian enters into the resurrected life of Christ (Quacquarelli 1973). But the font from which the new Christian is born is of course a womb – the womb of the Church[18] – and the new Christian is an *alter Christus*, another Christ, and a member of the body of Christ. The birth of the Christian from the font is thus analogous to the birth of Christ from his mother's womb. A prayer in a Visigothic prayer book of the eighth century (*Oracional de Verona*, Tarragona, 731: prayer 209) asks that the petitioners might enter the womb of the Virgin Mary so that she can present them to Christ in Heaven – as though re-birth to life in Christ means birth from his own mother's womb. So the number eight is associated with the Resurrection, and hence, we might surmise, with re-birth from Mary's womb.

In the Holy Land, the earliest octagonal building seems to have been the Church of the Holy Nativity, in Bethlehem.[19] This building enshrined the spot on which Mary gave birth to Christ. That building was destroyed and replaced by a larger basilica in the fifth century. However, recent archaeological excavations have uncovered another octagonal church, on the road from Jerusalem to Bethlehem. This is known at the *Kathisma* church, meaning the 'seat'.[20] The reason for this dedication is that it enshrines at its centre a stone upon which the pregnant Mary is said to have rested on her way to Bethlehem. The church seems to date from the fifth century, but after the Muslim conquest, it was turned into a mosque and subsequently was destroyed.

Both these buildings, then, are associated with Mary's pregnancy and childbearing – a motif which seems to be associated with Anglo-Saxon devotion to Agia Sophia.[21] So it may be that Norton is correct in identifying the earlier structure on the site of the York chapter house as Alcuin's church of Holy Wisdom, and that it was deliberately constructed to be a symbol of the woman

---

[18] The Anglo-Saxon font at Kilpeck, Herefordshire, is made explicitly in the form of a pregnant belly.
[19] Information given to me in conversation, by Rina Avner, of the Israel Antiquities Authority.
[20] The excavation was conducted by Rina Avner, and a thorough account of it is given in Shoemaker (2002, 81-98).
[21] Later Romanesque art also associated Wisdom with the Incarnation of the Word from Mary. A relief sculpture of the Adoration of the Magi, in Arezzo, and of the Virgin in Majesty, at Beaucaire, both include the legend, 'In gremio matris Sapientia Patris': 'The Wisdom of the Father in the lap of the mother' (Forsyth 1972, plates 1 and 2).

who was Wisdom's house, in order that Wisdom might be enshrined there.

Endnote: The origins of Mary's association with Wisdom

Hagia Sophia was, of course, the dedication of the principle church of Constantinople, and Christopher Norton has suggested that York's own association with the Emperor Constantine – York being the city in which he was proclaimed emperor – may account for the dedication of Archbishop Albert's church of Sophia (Norton, forthcoming). Margaret Barker, the biblical scholar, has suggested that Wisdom's association with the Virgin Mary goes back to New Testament times and was continued in the Eastern church in its early centuries (Barker 2003; Barker forthcoming). Her arguments have not been widely accepted amongst Patristic and Byzantine scholars; but even if she is correct, we still need to ask the question: how did the association of Mary with Wisdom arrive in Anglo-Saxon England? Bishop Acca, in whose tomb was the portable altar described above, was the devoted student and chaplain of Wilfrid (634-709/710), who has been credited with building the former church of St. Mary at Hexham, some time during or after 705. Twelfth-century descriptions suggest that it was polygonal, and modern scholars suggest that it may have been based on Arculph's description of the church at the site of the Virgin's tomb and assumption, in the Valley of Jehosaphat, near Jerusalem (Gem 1983, 11-12). In the light of the evidence for octagonal churches associated with Mary's childbearing, however, we should not rule out the possibility that Wilfrid knew of such buildings and that it was these which provided the model for his own Marian chapel. Perhaps it was also Wilfrid who introduced to England a distinctive cult of Christ as Holy Wisdom. Wilfrid's continental travels, and their effect upon his ecclesiastical policies and style of life, have been discussed by a number of scholars (Farmer 1974), but it would require new investigations to address the specific question of how likely it is that these were the source of Acca and Alcuin's devotion to Agia Sophia.

Bibliography

Allott, S. 1974. *Alcuin of York: His Life and Letters*, York: William Sessions (York)

Bailey, R.N. 1974. 'The Ango-Saxon metalwork from Hexham', in D.P. Kirby (ed.), *Saint Wilfrid at Hexham*, Oriel Press (Newcastle upon Tyne): 141-167

Barker, M. 2003. *The Great High Priest*, T&T Clark (London)

Barker, M. forthcoming. 'The life-giving spring', in C. Maunder (ed.), *The Origins of the Cult of the Virgin Mary*, Continuum (London)

Blair, P.H. 1964. 'Observations on the *Historia Regum*', in N.K.Chadwick (ed.), *Celt and Saxon: Studies in the Early British Border*, Cambridge

Boss, S.J. 2000. *Empress and Handmaid: On Nature and Gender in the Cult of the Virgin Mary*, Cassell (London)

Boss, S.J. 2004. *Mary*, New Century Theology series, Continuum (London)

Brown, S. 2003. *York Minster: An Architectural History, c.1220-1500*, English Heritage (Swindon)

Browne, J. 1847. *The History of the Metropolitan Church of St. Peter, York*, Longman & Co. (London, Oxford and Cambridge)

Budge, E.A.W. (ed. and trans.) 1910. 'A homily of Apa Basil ... concerning the end of the world and the Temple of Solomon, and the going forth from the body', in *Coptic Homilies in the Dialect of Upper Egypt, edited from the Papyrys Codex Oriental 5001 in the British Museum*, British Museum (London): 245-257

Bullough, D.A. 2002. *Alcuin: Achievement and Reputation*, Brill (Leiden)

Catta, E., 1961. 'Sedes sapientiae', in H. du Manoir (ed.), *Maria: Etudes sur la Vierge Marie*, Vol.6, Beauchesne (Paris): 689-866

Cannon, J. 2006. 'Gothic remodelling itself? Restoration and intention at the Outer North Porch of St Mary Redcliffe, Bristol', unpublished paper.

Clayton, M. 1990. *The Cult of the Virgin Mary in Anglo-Saxon England*, Cambridge University Press (Cambridge)

Dawton, N. 1990. 'The York chapter house: notes on the trumeau Virgin and the iconographic significance of the building', in H. Weston and D. Davies (eds.), *Essays in Honour of John White*, University College London (London): 48-54

[Eadmer] 1904. *Eadmeri Monachi Cantuariensis Tractatus de Conceptione Sanctae Mariae*, H. Thurston and T. Slater (eds.), Herder (Freiburg-im-Breisgau)

Farmer, D.H. 1974. 'Saint Wilfrid', in D.P. Kirby (ed.), *Saint Wilfrid at Hexham*, Oriel Press (Newcastle upon Tyne): 35-59.

Forsyth, I. 1972. *Throne of Wisdom: Wood Sculptures of the Madonna in Romanesque France*, Princeton University Press (Princeton, NJ)

Foussard, M. 1971. '*Aulae Sidereae*: Vers de Jean Scot au Roi Charles: introduction, texte, traduction et notes', in A. Grabar and J. Hubert (eds.), *Cahiers Archéologiques*, 21. Editions Klincksieck (Paris): 79-88

Frénaud, Dom, G. 1961. 'Le culte de Notre Dame dans l'ancienne liturgie Latine', in H. du Manoir (ed.), *Maria: Etudes sur la Vierge Marie*, Vol.6, Beauchesne (Paris): 157-211

Gem, R. 1983. 'Towards an iconography of Anglo-Saxon architecture', *Journal of the Warburg and Courtauld Institutes*, 46: 1-18

Herren, M. 1987. 'Eriugena's "Aulae Sidereae", the "Codex Aureus", and the Palatine Church of St. Mary at Compiègne', in *Studi Medievali*, third series, 28 (2): 593-608

Krautheimer, R. 1969. *Studies in Early Christian, Medieval, and Renaissance Art*, University of London Press (London)

Meyers, R. 1995. 'The Wisdom of God and the Word of God: Alcuin's mass "Of Wisdom"', in M. Dudley (ed.), *Like a Two-Edged Sword: The Word of God in Liturgy and History (Essays in honour of Canon Donald Gray)*, Canterbury Press (Norwich): 39-59

Morris, R. 1986. 'Alcuin, York and the *alma Sophia*', in L.A.S. Butler and R.K. Morris (eds.), *The Anglo-Saxon Church: Papers on History, Architecture, and Archaeology in Honour of Dr. H.M. Taylor*, Council for British Archaeology, Research Report 60 (London)

Norton, C. 1998. 'The Anglo-Saxon cathedral at York and the topography of the Anglian city', *Journal of the British Archaeological Association*, 151: 1-42

Norton, C. forthcoming. 'Alcuin's York', in M. Garrison (ed.), *Alcuin*, Cambridge University Press (Cambridge)

O'Carroll, M. 1982. *Theotokos: A Theological Encyclopedia of the Blessed Virgin Mary*, Dominican Publications (Dublin)

Quacquarelli, A. 1973. *L'Ogdoade Patristica e suoi Riflessi nella Liturgia e nei Monumenti (Quaderni de "Vetera Christianorum", 7)*, Adriatica Editrice (Bari)

Salter, H.E. 1929. *Facsimiles of Early Charters in Oxford Muniment Rooms*, Oxford

Shoemaker, S. 2002. *Ancient Traditions of the Virgin Mary's Dormition and Assumption*, Oxford University Press (Oxford)

Thompson, A.H. 1947. 'The Chapel of St. Mary and the Holy Angels, otherwise known as St. Sepulchre's Chapel, at York', *Yorkshire Archaeological Journal*, 36: 63-77

Tudor-Craig, P. 2002. 'The iconography of Wisdom and the frontispiece to the *Bible Historiale*, British Library, Additional Manuscript 18856', in C.M. Barron and J. Stratford (eds.), *The Church and Learning in Later Medieval Society: Essays in Honour of R.B. Dobson (Proceedings of the 1999 Harlaxton Symposium)*, Shaun Tyas (Donington): 110-127

Vieillard-Troïekouroff, M. 1971. 'La chapelle du palais de Charles le Chauve à Compiègne', in *Cahiers Archéologiques*, 21 Editions Klincksieck (Paris): 89-108

Approaching Interdisciplinarity

Zoë L. Devlin

The papers presented in this volume represent an attempt to further our understanding of the early medieval period in the British Isles through the combination of both historical (i.e. documentary) and archaeological sources. In organising this conference, our aim was to create an environment in which we could demonstrate the importance of interdisciplinary work by presenting examples of new research and discussing the practical issues surrounding it in the hope of establishing a way forward for interdisciplinary studies, which has been often undermined by disciplinary divisions. Both the conference papers and the ensuing discussion raised a number of issues that are of concern for researchers engaged in interdisciplinary studies in general and for those at the start of their career in particular.

The conference was primarily intended to give current and recent research students a venue to discuss their interdisciplinary research and the issues they had encountered, with more experienced researchers, in particular Alex Woolf, on hand to discuss these issues. As we were determined that all papers should be genuinely interdisciplinary, rather than for instance using archaeology to illustrate and support historical reasoning, we began by seeking out and inviting research students using both history and archaeology to give papers. One major issue that arose immediately was the comparative lack of junior researchers engaged in interdisciplinary projects. This seems to have a great deal to do with the inherent divisions between the disciplines in universities. Few universities seem to actively promote interdisciplinary study at doctoral level and the divisions between departments – in most cases housed in separate buildings with entirely separate academic staff – effectively militate against it. Even where the facilities and will for interdisciplinary research and supervision exist, as at the Centre for Medieval Studies in York where the conference organisers were based, there are far greater numbers of doctoral candidates undertaking interdisciplinary research in the disciplines of History and English, or History and French, than there are in History and Archaeology.

This disciplinary divide is clearly well-entrenched by the time students reach doctoral level. The relatively small number of students engaged in research using both historical and archaeological sources suggests that most either feel they lack the skills for, or have little interest in pursuing, such a project. This can only be a product of their undergraduate and Masters' training. When I began my undergraduate degree in Archaeology and Medieval History at the University of Sheffield in 1997, it seemed obvious to me that the two disciplines should rightly work together to produce the fullest understanding possible of the past. However, it quickly became clear that this view was not necessarily shared by academics themselves and that the disciplines were effectively two entirely separate entities (see also Woolf and Capper, this volume). That such a division should be so clear to an undergraduate is illustrative of how widely accepted it had become generally across both disciplines. Personal observation, as both a student and more recently as Graduate Teaching Assistant and lecturer, has suggested that the already small numbers of undergraduate students enrolling on interdisciplinary courses tend to decline during the first year of study as many switch to a single honours degree in one or other of their subjects. Often this may be down to a stronger interest in one subject or a greater familiarity with one already studied at A level, but it may also be partly the result of feelings of confusion regarding the differing academic demands of two separate disciplines or, worse, a lack of coherence between the differing programmes resulting in the idea that they have incompatible approaches and methodologies. After all, students tend to be required to take a mix of modules developed for each single honours degree programme rather than modules designed to incorporate the two. Students can also perceive joint degrees as more work, requiring them to learn the methods, histories and theories of two disciplines rather than just the one that many of their peers need to get to grips with. Altogether, with a general lack of undergraduate teaching specifically on interdisciplinary methods meaning that students have few role models and little personal experience in this area, it is hardly surprising that doctoral candidates have a strong tendency to choose a single-discipline research project.

Theory and politics

Much has been written on the nature of the relationship between history and archaeology and there have been many suggestions as to how a fruitful dialogue might be achieved or as to how a single interdisciplinary methodology might be developed (for bibliographies and reviews, see Halsall 1997, 817-827; and the content of *Archaeological Review from Cambridge* 14 (1); for more recent examples of explicit attempts at establishing a methodology, see Carver 2002; Moreland 2003; for a review of recent works incorporating historical and archaeological evidence, see Hills 2007; see also Capper and Woolf, this volume). Despite this though, a completely effective means of interdisciplinary collaboration has yet to be established. Both Capper and Woolf here make the point very clearly that the tendency for practitioners of one discipline to misuse the evidence and methods of the other has undermined the relationship between the two, as has the inevitable criticism and complaints that follow. Training is the major issue here – it's all too easy to forget the number of years spent learning to work within your own discipline and to take theories and evidence from another uncritically and without fully understanding them. As Capper and Woolf indicate, this creates a professional atmosphere in which people are potentially mistrustful of the ways in which their work may be used by practitioners of the other discipline, reducing opportunities for cross-discipline collaboration and dialogue. The implication is that the path to interdisciplinarity can be found not in arguing about theoretical balance and who sets the research agenda, and not in finding a methodology that lies somewhere between the two disciplines, but in admitting the limits of individual knowledge and actively creating opportunities for exchanging ideas and sharing developments between different specialists.

Practical aspects of interdisciplinary research

The range of knowledge and skills required to undertake interdisciplinary work is an important issue that comes out of the papers by Woolf, Capper and Holas-Clark. This was a major concern in particular for the doctoral candidates presenting at the conference. As Capper comments, the really successful examples of interdisciplinary projects are those published by scholars with many years' experience in their chosen fields – research of a scale and quality that a doctoral candidate might aspire to but cannot reasonably expect to achieve at a period in their career when they are still learning about their discipline(s) and developing their skills. Caroline Holas-Clark also comments on how a successful interdisciplinary approach to the study of the past can only really result from many years' study. Skills development is of crucial importance for all doctoral candidates, most of whom will have to learn aspects of source analysis that are not taught at undergraduate level, such as palaeography or numismatics. Both Capper and Holas-Clark comment on their own experience of how learning new skills impacted upon the time management of their projects. In order to be able to fully analyse and critique the sources used, the scope of the interdisciplinary PhD research project may have to be reduced to allow the time to learn the necessary skills. This is likely to be the case regardless of whether or not the individual has a pre-doctoral interdisciplinary background, as undertaking a combined degree necessarily reduces the range of modules from each discipline that can be studied. PhD students conducting an interdisciplinary research project may well require a greater range of skills training than those operating within a single discipline and much of this may need to be self-taught depending upon the support mechanisms and range of expertise in place in the individual's home department. This is one of the areas where well-established support networks, as suggested by Capper, would be of great help to students, enabling them to discuss areas of their research with peers who may have more training in a given area. The need for PhD students to network is well-known but doctoral research continues to be a largely solitary occupation. The establishment of cross-departmental and cross-institutional networks would be a potential source of support in the acquisition of new skills and the learning of new theories, with students discussing ideas and suggesting sources of information to each other.

Capper and Holas-Clark also describe the other factors that inevitably impact upon the management of interdisciplinary research projects. By increasing the range of evidence studied it is necessary to reduce the scope of the research in other ways, by covering a shorter period of time or a smaller geographical area. This is especially the case for PhD students, whose research is necessarily curtailed to a maximum of four years full-time by funding bodies and institutional targets. It is also a major issue, though, for the more established scholar considering an interdisciplinary research project. Again, research funding will carry its own time-scale restrictions but there are other factors to consider too, such as the need to produce high quality publications for the RAE process as well as to establish a research profile in order to secure promotion and a 'name' within their discipline. This, coupled with other demands on their time related to teaching and administrative work, may mean that scholars are less inclined to undertake a large-scale interdisciplinary project, especially if incorporating material from more than one discipline means compromising other aspects of the research plan. Capper is right to argue that an interdisciplinary approach to a research topic is something that has to be justified, not just to ensure that such an approach adds something of value to our understanding of a particular topic, but also to ensure that it is worth what we may potentially lose.

Methodology

As mentioned above, there have been suggestions that developing a specifically interdisciplinary methodology to the study of the past might create a productive dialogue between historians and archaeologists and combat the problems that arise as a result of a lack of training in both disciplines. This idea has so far proved unsuccessful and the papers in this volume would seem to argue against such an approach. The papers by Boss, Garcia, Greene, Reed and myself all approach their subjects from the point of view that an interdisciplinary approach can reveal more about the past than either discipline can do alone. However, each analyses the evidence according to the paradigms of the individual discipline and combines the results of this to create an argument about social and cultural life in early medieval Britain. For Sharon A. Greene and myself, the evidence from documentary sources has led to a reanalysis of the archaeological evidence and a new explanation for behaviour in the past. My own paper discussed how the evidence from Anglo-Saxon wills enables us to understand the context in which changes in burial practices occurred, potentially providing a new explanation for changes in attitudes to the dead at this time. Greene's reanalysis of documentary sources' references to off-shore islands allows her to critique the assumptions that many archaeologists have held about their habitation, providing the context for a greater understanding of place in early medieval Ireland. It is arguable that such an analysis is only possible because of the contemporary viewpoint provided by the documentary sources. The papers by Boss, Garcia and Reed all draw together evidence from history and archaeology to create a fuller picture of their subjects. Sarah Boss' use of ecclesiastical texts enables her to argue persuasively in support of what architectural and archaeological evidence can only hint at: the location of Alcuin's church dedicated to Alma Sophia in York. At the same time, understanding the architectural background to this and similar churches provides a physical context for the worship of Mary and Holy Wisdom that is revealed by the textual sources. Michael Garcia's paper effectively demonstrates that while both archaeological and documentary evidence for the survival of Christian cult centres in Britain beyond the Roman withdrawal is sparse, combining the evidence from both enables a more thorough and conscientious analysis of both types of material and allows us to draw conclusions that would not be possible with a single-discipline approach. Finally, Michael F. Reed draws together the results of analyses within archaeological and art-historical approaches and the contextual evidence of documentary sources to construct a compelling picture of the structure and culture of lordship in Anglo-Scandinavian Suffolk. All these approaches therefore indicate that an interdisciplinary approach can potentially reveal more about the past than can the evidence from a single discipline. However, this can only be revealed to us by adopting the methodologies appropriate for the particular type of evidence, rather than attempting to create a new interdisciplinary approach. This combines well with Capper's argument that we should not try to break down disciplinary divides and develop a single interdisciplinary methodology as research questions are defined by disciplinarity. Rather, we should be looking for areas in which the different disciplines have complementary research questions and using the results of both to inform the other and to reveal new information that cannot be arrived at through single-discipline analysis.

However, this does not necessarily mean maintaining the structural and cultural divide between historians and archaeologists. It has been demonstrated already that this divide effectively discourages the development of new interdisciplinary researchers. Woolf's paper advocates that we should think of ourselves as groups of specialists rather than as two distinct disciplines, with those specialisms crossing discipline boundaries rather than maintaining them. Such an approach has a great deal to recommend it, not least by enabling the recognition of similar areas of research interest such as the economy, where both archaeologists and historians have similar approaches. In addition, the idea of strict distinctions between the disciplines of history and archaeology cannot always be maintained, as there are many sub-disciplines and other related external disciplines that inform our studies. For example, numismatics (Capper, Holas-Clark) is a small but highly specialised sub-discipline not directly taught in many undergraduate programmes; art-history (Boss, Reed) is often subsumed within departments of archaeology and/or architecture with a related developmental history and theoretical background; and the study of standing architecture (Boss) is practised by archaeologists as often as by architectural historians. Other disciplines such as philology (Woolf) and sociology and anthropology (Devlin) are also called upon for the study of the past by both archaeologists and historians, who are in danger of misusing those disciplines as often as each others' (cf. Capper). Interdisciplinarity can therefore not limit itself to just the two disciplines of archaeology and history but can potentially call upon a range of expertise in attempting to understand human behaviour. The problems caused by a faulty understanding of each others' disciplines has already been commented upon. If it is hard for archaeologists and historians to fully comprehend two disciplines, it is so much harder for them to understand three, four or even more. Capper discusses the benefits of a collaborative approach to interdisciplinary studies, which follows Woolf's recommendation by bringing together a group of people with individual yet complementary specialisms, and overcomes the idea that a single person has to possess the broad base of knowledge necessary to undertake effective interdisciplinary work. A collaborative approach may well prove to be a fruitful one, but it is also one which brings a number of its own problems and concerns, as Capper discusses. However, it may well prove to be a beneficial approach that enables the many problems encountered by single scholars undertaking interdisciplinary work to be overcome.

Conclusion

Previous discussions of the relationship between history and archaeology have tended to focus on the theoretical aspects and have often been coloured by the adversarial stance taken by some of the participants. This volume attempts to overcome the problems thrown up by this history of encounters by considering the practical aspects of interdisciplinarity. It is clear that interdisciplinary work cannot be undertaken for its own sake but instead must have a particular research agenda that can only be achieved by combining the approaches of both disciplines. To be worthwhile, it needs to be more than the sum of its parts. However, a specific interdisciplinary methodology does not seem to be an appropriate way forward. Practitioners must be skilled in the approaches of both disciplines, whether individually or as part of a collaborative team, and it is the results of the combined approach that should be seen as special, rather than the methodology used to get there.

At present, there are a number of barriers to interdisciplinary work, most related to the structure of universities and degree programmes, which socialise students into specific disciplines. Teaching constraints within single discipline programmes and the general lack of interdisciplinary modules means few students get the opportunity to learn about the interdisciplinary research their lecturers might be undertaking, which may be difficult to incorporate fully into single-discipline teaching. Undergraduate and most postgraduate training programmes therefore inevitably lead to a lack of skilled practitioners for interdisciplinary work and many doctoral candidates and established scholars alike need to be self-motivated in selecting and gaining the skills to undertake such a project.

The selection of an interdisciplinary research project at doctoral level also has potential implications for the future, especially for the career path of the individual researcher. The issue of employability was a major area of concern that arose during the discussion at the end of the conference. Even at institutions where there is an active interest in the research and teaching of interdisciplinary studies, individuals are still hired and paid for by single-discipline departments whose main concern is not surprisingly to hire people who can teach their discipline and who have research plans that will fit well within the department. While having a foot in both camps may initially appear to be an asset, the concern is that a truly interdisciplinary background may result in the candidate appearing as neither one thing nor the other, as too much of an historian for an archaeology department and too archaeological for a history department. All this suggests that interdisciplinary research is not something that can be undertaken lightly and requires very high quality support from the host institution and the wider network of researchers. However, the range of skills acquired and the evidence examined means that interdisciplinary research can bring its own rewards in terms of personal enjoyment and development.

Interdisciplinary approaches are still relatively rare within history and archaeology but their potential is enormous. The tendency to see history and archaeology as opposing factions vying for theoretical control has largely prevented the development of collaborative approaches to date. This volume has demonstrated that interdisciplinary research projects are possible without undermining either discipline or imposing the theoretical dominance of one over the other. With the intensity of the debate subsiding since the end of the 1990s, now would be an ideal time to reinstate communication between the two sides and create a new way of approaching interdisciplinarity.

Bibliography

Carver, C. 2002. 'Marriages of true minds: archaeology with texts', in B. Cunliffe, W. Davies and C. Renfrew (eds.), *Archaeology: the Widening Debate*, Oxford University Press (Oxford): 465-94

Halsall, G. 1997. 'Archaeology and historiography', in M. Bentley (ed.), *Companion to Historiography*, Routledge (London & New York): 805-27

Hills, C. 2007. 'History and archaeology: the state of play in early medieval Europe', *Antiquity*, 81: 191-200

Moreland, J. 2003. *Archaeology and Text*, Gerald Duckworth and Co Ltd (London)

www.ingramcontent.com/pod-product-compliance
Ingram Content Group UK Ltd.
Pitfield, Milton Keynes, MK11 3LW, UK
UKHW061213180426
11947UKWH00029B/2019